northern lights

High Strangeness in Sweden

Fred Andersson

BEYOND THE FRAY
Publishing

Published by Beyond The Fray Publishing

ISBN 13: 978-1-954528-72-7

Cover design: Disgruntled Dystopian Publications

Beyond The Fray Publishing, a division of Beyond The Fray, LLC, San Diego, CA
www.beyondthefraypublishing.com

BEYOND THE FRAY
Publishing

contents

This book is dedicated to experiencers everywhere.

The woo is the clue
The pebble in your shoe
There is little one can do
Trust me, it's more True
It is a universal glue
That changes your point of view
On all you thought you knew.

-Allen H. Greenfield

introduction

"He looks like an alien," my mother whispered in that cold, sterile waiting hall at the Östersund bus station during the early '90s. I looked at the man speaking and pointing at blurry photos in front of a small audience. Yeah, there was something otherworldly about him: oddly shaped face, slightly bulging eyes, and a forehead not of this earth. To be honest, he reminded me more of Rowan Atkinson's character Mr. Bean than a visitor from another planet.

I don't remember the exact year and date, but somehow I had convinced my dear mother to join me in listening to a lecture held by *UFO-Z* in a bus station waiting room! Our family was at the time active members of an evangelical congregation, Pingstkyrkan, and the concept of visitors from outer space wasn't exactly compatible with our church's agenda. What probably made the whole thing even more embarrassing for my mother was that the lecture area was in front of the huge waiting hall window —where everyone in our small town could see us. To be seen at such an event would be very... dare I say, scandalous?

I've always been a weird kid. Maybe the result of escaping into a world of imagination when my own and my family's life was, to say the least, complicated and downright terrible at times. So the idea of something mysterious out there, the unknown and unexplainable, attracted me a lot more than any earthly matters. I was (and still am) one of those chubby little nerds with glasses who always hung around the esoteric shelves at the library, looking for new and old books about mysterious disappearances, UFOs, spontaneous combustion (it was so present in the stuff I read, I thought it was the most common cause of death for a while), ghosts, and other things not normally respected or believed in our "normal" world. It didn't help that one of the librarians, an elderly lady with a strict, old-fashioned hair bun, told me children disappeared in the dimly lit basement of her library.

One of my earlier memories was getting a worn-out copy of Eugene Semitjov's *De Otroliga Tefaten* (*The Incredible Saucers*), first out in 1974, a UFO book jam-packed with photos and stories. Semitjov was a very skilled illustrator and journalist specializing in popular science. One fascination he had was the mystery of flying saucers. He wrote many books, several on this subject. However, *De Otroliga Tefaten* stood out for me—maybe because it had a quite skeptical view of the phenomenon. For example, he begins the book with a photo of a fleet of UFOs over Stockholm and later reveals it's a hoax he made to prove how easy it is to fake photographic evidence. In the book, he examines some of the most interesting cases at the time (including Lonnie Zamora's 1964 encounter in Socorro, New Mexico—still a personal favorite), interviews witnesses, and manages to balance perfectly on the edge of skepticism and an open mind.

I am definitely not a debunker. Let's call myself an open-minded skeptic. A debunker to me is someone who has a belief, a belief they do everything to prove is right. And to be honest, that's not better than being someone who uncritically believes in everything out of the ordinary. Why even believe in everything? There won't be any mysteries left to explore!

I'm forever grateful for what Eugene Semitjov introduced to me, and from time to time—just like in this very moment—I have the book beside me, reminding me of the mysterious universe we live in.

With *Northern Lights: High Strangeness in Sweden*, I would like to bring out the weirdness of this cold, dark country (at least during the winter months) in a book where I will share some incredible stories—many of them which have never reached outside Sweden. My focus is on humanoids and UFOs, but I promise that there will also be other kinds of high strangeness between these pages. I admit I am more interested in the experiences told by the witnesses than physical proof. I have not ventured out to do any field investigations or focused on trying to find natural, more logical explanations (though I speculate a bit in some of the chapters). It's all about the stories.

I prefer using the expression "high strangeness," as it fits the stories—and I like to call them stories—that trigger my interest. There is something with the presence of extraordinary inside the out of the ordinary that makes me feel awake. Are they folklore, dreams, hoaxes, or rooted in some kind of outer or inner reality? I don't know, and to be honest, I don't care.

Storytelling is as old as mankind, an important way to transfer information, knowledge, and wisdom through the generations. Sometimes it might lack apparent wisdom—at least on the surface. But what it brings is the message of imagination, humor, and individuality. It's all about highly personal experiences where the individual gains something from it—may it be terror, enlightenment, or even amusement.

I see the phenomenon as a blank canvas, and those who can sense it as artists flinging colors onto the invisible surface, creating patterns, motives, and events. The creation—the result—is partly ourselves, and the rest is the texture of the goblin world shaping the experience. It might be nonsense, but it's our nonsense.

The main focus in this fringe subject has always been on the United States, the United Kingdom, France, and other bigger territories. The majority of the literature published in the English language deals with cases and opinions regarding these countries, and even though I love that, it can be quite tedious hearing the same stories over and over again. There's so much more to be explored! I couldn't have written this book without the existence of UFO-Sverige, the main organization in Sweden that deals with unexplained lights in the skies, humanoid encounters, abductions, and flying saucer landings on dark country roads. Most of their case files up until 2004 are stored at the humongous Archives for the Unexplained in Norrköping, a one-of-a-kind source for research regarding the phenomenon (support them by going to their homepage and ordering some books or magazines: http://www.afu.se/). Through them, I've received a lot of help.

UFO-Sverige's publishing of magazines, from *UFO-Information* in the '70s to the current *UFO-Aktuellt*, has been very valuable to my research, with a huge amount of reports of high (and not so high) strangeness of all kinds.

Deeply involved in UFO-Sverige is Clas Svahn, who has written a couple of excellent books on the subject: *Mötet i Gläntan: Sveriges mest Kända Närkontakt med UFO* (Parthenon, 1995), *UFO-Mysteriet: Från Flygande Tefat till Cirklar i Sädesfält* (Parthenon, 1998), and *UFO: Spökraketer, Ljusglober och Utomjordingar* (Parthenon, 2014). All available in Swedish only.

Before I proceed, I'd like to mention a few names that are important for the creation of this book: Anders Liljegren at Archives for the Unexplained, whose patience with me has been extraordinary; Håkan Blomqvist for additional information and clearing up the facts regarding the chapter "Night of the UFOs"; Paul A. J. Lewis for grammar check and valuable comments regarding the same chapter; Dr. Patrick Jonsson for his kindness and knowledge regarding both the case and the esoteric viewpoint on ufology; UFO-Sverige for being a wonderful source of information, wisdom, and knowledge; Idgie Ljunggren, Martin Lindberg, and Milly Nilsson for their support and comments on all the mumbo jumbo I've sent them during the writing of this book; Markus Widegren and Clara Lidner for the pentagram and snail (good pub name!); Pux, Vuk/*Tracing Owls*, and Theo Paijmans for their support; David Moore and John E. L. Tenney for valuable comments and inspiration; Allan H. Greenfield for the wisdom and the wonderful poem; Jenny Randles and Jacques Vallée for the kind permission to use quotes from their books; Rob Kristoffersen/*Our Strange Skies* and Ryan Sprague/*Somewhere in the Skies* for being great inspirations; Joel Bergling, a beloved friend; and Grzegorz, for the love and proofreading.

I'm very grateful for the witnesses, the heroes of this book, who wanted to talk to me about their experiences. And all those on Twitter who have followed my journey with this book.

Northern Lights: High Strangeness in Sweden deals mainly with UFOs and aliens, but there are a few stories that stray away from those subjects. I feel it's necessary to show the variety of the phenomena in our little country. So stuff your Fjällräven backpacks with hot chocolate, lussebullar, cinnamon buns, tunnbrödrulle, warm clothes, and join me in the world of strangeness. Sweden is a lot wilder than you'd think.

Fred Andersson
2023-02-17

one
watch out, it's not human!

AT THE END of the unfairly criticized *Friday the 13th* sequel *Jason X*, two overaged teenagers are making out at the edge of a lake and witness a glowing object entering the atmosphere and crashing down into the woods. They turn to each other and say, "Let's take a look!" The screen fades to black, and the credits roll on yet another chapter of the endless series in the slasher saga about Jason Voorhees.

It's a reference to many sci-fi movies of the past, where either an old loner in the forest finds an alien glob and pokes at it with a stick, or teenagers witness a strange light in the sky and see it as a new great adventure to explore (and probably have premarital sex and smoke weed)—and it never ends well. The legend says magpies and crows (but there's no empirical evidence for it) are attracted to shiny, glittering objects, and maybe we humans feel the same curiosity when we see lights or something bright where it shouldn't be? It's both a sense of comfort, "we're not alone, someone else is here," and fear if the light is where it's not supposed to be, let's say in an abandoned building or in your own, empty basement.

Lights are signs of living stuff, maybe intelligent, and we're too curious not to check what the heck it is. Okay, let me correct myself: maybe we're more like moths than birds after all, but instead of stubbornly bumping our heads into lamps, we're looking for what's beyond our own worldly existence? Maybe that's one reason UFOs have lights, to make us aware of them?

In the case I'm going to go into now, the setup is similar: two teens, one dark evening, and foolish youthful curiosity that ends up in pure terror. After all, haven't we all been there?

The year is 1967, August 23, and the location is the community of Åby. The young heroes of the story, let's call them Maria and Peter (they've always asked to be anonymous, and I intend to keep it that way), two fifteen-year-old kids, were out strolling one evening. It was 8 p.m. when they noticed a faint, eerie red light near the treetops. It was moving slowly, without any clear shape, and seemed to land near the edge of a forest.

A creepy, uncomfortable feeling of not being alone struck them, and they decided to head back home, away from the noiseless, eerie glow. The uncomfortable feeling stayed with them all the way... and would soon transcend into pure horror.

Almost home, Maria was overcome by her teenage curiosity and, in the company of Peter, returned to the location. She wanted to study the light phenomenon even more. To their surprise, it was still there, once again above the treetops, but this time moving back and forth until it headed east and disappeared. They were now near an abandoned, padlocked cabin, and now it started to get really scary.

Something was moving inside the small house. Yellow, ghostly lights visible through the window were floating in one of the rooms—and on the outside, shining against the wall of the cabin, a cone of light was seemingly coming up from the ground. A vague, thumping sound was heard, as if someone was knocking on a piece of wood. Maria and Peter later described the atmosphere as unreal and frightening, and it was about to get even worse.

The red light appeared again, this time coming in from the west. While moving at the same leisurely speed as earlier, the color was changing from red to white and back again several times, until it once again seemingly landed on a nearby field.

All of this was too much for the kids, and they headed back to safety as fast as possible. At least, they thought it was safe. The peculiar feeling of being observed and not being alone was still with them. First, they tried to get into Peter's home, but his parents didn't answer the doorbell and their desperate knocks. Instead, they continued to another nearby house where his sisters lived.

Suddenly, a strong light appeared above them, approximately three meters up. It reminded them of a giant flashlight shining down with a strong, central source that was very difficult to explain. A sharp, whistling sound was heard. The kids had difficulty explaining how it sounded, but imagine placing a straw of grass between your hands and blowing through it (high-pitched sounds are not unusual to be heard during experiences like this, and some say it's not a good sign). Sounds of fast, intensive footsteps were heard, with pauses between each series of steps. It seemed to come from the stream not far away, and Maria—in her infinite teenage wisdom—took the brave decision to take a closer look, with Peter huddling right behind her.

At first, she thought it was a friend of hers, but within seconds Peter grabbed her arm and pulled her back while screaming, "Watch out, it's not human!" This wasn't a friend; it was a creature not of this earth. It had jumped up at them on light legs and was now standing dimly lit with a trembling body. The creature was short, around 130 centimeters. Its head was bigger than what one would expect from a child, either covered with dark hair or a tight hoodie with a peak going down in between the eyes, and dressed in what looked like a dark overall. At the height of the ankles, cords were attached, which flashed a bright light for a short moment.

The eyes were big and dark, but as the creature had its head slightly down, it was difficult to see any details. Where the mouth should be, there was something like a cross, an X. This particular detail is interesting because it might also have been a slit-shaped nose and mouth meeting each other at the tips. Standing still, Maria and Peter noticed how its movements were shivering, shaking, either from nervous insecurity or trembling from adrenaline.

While studying the tough-looking little visitor, they saw how it raised its arms. In its left hand, it held an object, a box attached to a handle, with a tube sticking out at the front. Peter noticed an arch of light at the top of the tube. It almost looked like a weapon.

Scared out of their minds, the teenagers ran to the house of Peters sisters and to safety. Both families could verify how Maria and Peter were genuinely upset from their experience, and in the days after, they preferred to stay inside after dark. Perfectly understandable if you ask me.

The encounter with the creature itself is fascinating, but it's the events before it that make this stand out, particularly the paranormal aspect: the haunted cabin. During my work with the paranormal show *Det Okända*," I interviewed many witnesses, and I noticed that after the interviews, conversations often opened up to things beyond traditional paranormal experiences such as ghosts and poltergeists. Stories about strange lights in the sky, gnome-like critters appearing suddenly, and a strong sense of being psychically connected to other people and foreseeing the future were also discussed, and the power to heal friends and family was always present. One woman described how she met a huge troll on the second floor of her house, and a young man told me about lights floating above the forest near his family's countryside villa.

According to a skeptical research paper, "Recent systematic research by Basterfield and Thalbourne has confirmed anecdotal reports of higher levels of paranormal belief and reports of ostensibly paranormal experiences among those claiming alien contact" ("Psychological Aspects of the Alien Contact Experience," 2008). It seems to be common ground that one thing does not exclude the other. Several paranormal investigators focusing on subjects such as UFOs, cryptozoology, and ghosts have mentioned how it's always important to ask if anything else happened before, during, and after the event. More often than not, there's more to the story than just a hovering UFO or a hairy beast hiding behind some bushes. It's said that those who easily appreciate and enjoy magic illusions have a higher tendency to experience something out of the ordinary. It's like a mind that's open to the impossible and has a higher degree of seeing and experiencing paranormal, otherworldly, or downright mysterious phenomena. The illusion becomes the key, and the real-life trickster opens the path to another realm. In 1972, the Toronto Society for Psychical Research conducted the now-famous Philip experiment under the supervision of parapsychologist and mathematics professor George Owen and Dr. Joel Whitton. The experiment was constructed like a traditional séance, and at the beginning, it was not successful—not until its members tried a different approach.

In his book *The Hidden Universe*, Anthony Peake discusses an experiment overseen by psychologist Dr. Joel Whitton and devised by mathematician A. R. G. Owen, who was the director of the Toronto Society for Psychical Research and the husband of Iris Owen. According to Peake, Whitton argued on television that the group had achieved a "child-like creativity" by engaging in playful and humorous activities, including repetitive singing. Peake also notes that the experiment involved setting aside the orthodox adult mindset that "this cannot be done."

In an email conversation between me and legendary occultist and ufologist Allen H. Greenfield on the subject of contactees and experiencers, he writes *"Trance channeled 'contacts' are part of the tradition of trance mediumship and ancient oracle centers, but I think the 'physical' cases may be fleshed out from paranormal experiences. Both can, of course, be hoaxes, but mostly they seem as straight up as the percepients can be. I see the various 'fringe' phenomena as part of a broader pattern, and include paranormal phenomena (psi), Near Death Experiences, apparitions, elves and the Fae, cryptozoological phenomena and UFO-related cases, among others. My current thinking is that human perception is more limited than the phenomena, which originates perhaps in something like the Many Worlds Interpretation of Quantum Mechanics."*

Like the double-slit experiment indicates, our interaction with the quantum field affects the outcome of our intentions. The pattern Greenfield mentions is like waves, or rings on water. If you drop a stone in the water, it will create a series of waves spreading out in all directions. My guess is that those who can experience the paranormal have the ability to, so to speak, drop the stone and set the waves in motion.

The idea that those who are willingly entertained by magic tricks have a bigger chance of experiencing phenomena that can be called real magic is interesting. There is often a relationship between experiencers, contactees, those with a high interest in UFOs, the paranormal, and science fiction. By having a deep, almost profound view of the genre aspects of literature, movies, and art, they might also have a higher chance of actually experiencing out-of-the-ordinary things. It's like magic tricks and genre fiction; both deal with illusions of the impossible, weird, strange, and unlikely—and being open-minded to one of them often transcends into the other. It's a pathway to Magonia, one can say.

In the case of Maria and Peter, it's known that Peter had an interest in science fiction and UFOs. He talked and read about stuff in the genre and was the person who planted the idea that it was some kind of nonhuman entity they met during the incident. I'd say that Peter worked as a pathway here, being enthusiastic about his interest, bringing it up with Maria, and somehow they both got sucked into the world of the weird for two hours that night.

The paranormal activity continued around the house of the sisters for two nights, with unexplained clicking sounds outside, a similar light as the teenagers saw outside during their experience, ghostly footsteps, and other kinds of unexplainable noises. Someone—or something—had also damaged the window shutters at a time when the lights were on inside and, therefore, would not have attracted a typical burglar.

Of course, one can say it was two teenagers scaring themselves and their family through auto-suggestion, which is easily done—we've all been there. Nevertheless, in this case, there's more to be said, both in terms of physical evidence and memory.

The day after, in the comfort of sunlight, the family found strange bite marks on their apples, like an animal with small, oddly placed teeth had cut the apple open and tasted it. There were also remains of mucus on the fruits. Two different sets of footprints were found: one with three pointy toes, twenty-five centimeters in length, and one with two sections, like a heel and front, five centimeters in length.

I will go into Swedish folklore more later in the book you're holding, but let's take a pause and look at the subject in connection with what Maria and Peter experienced. Little people in the shape of elves, fairies, trolls, gnomes, and other kinds of tiny beings have been in the realm of folklore throughout the ages, especially in Sweden. Stories about them often belong to the mythology around farms, farming, and old houses. These little critters can be both helpers if you treat them right, or tricksters if you're not treating them or the farm in a good way.

In the old days, it happened that families moved from their farms just to please the original inhabitants of the area. The critter our teenagers met had a threatening attitude, to say the least, and scared them for days and weeks afterward just by showing itself (and to be fair, it seemed like a very scary incident). That's quite rare in our age. Friendliness, though sometimes with a sinister motive, is a lot more common. In 1973, Helge Eriksson told investigator and researcher (and co-founder of Archives for the Unexplained) Anders Liljegren about a strange event that took place in 1931, outside Eslöv, in southern Sweden.

It was early January, not long after New Year's Eve, when the twenty-three-year-old Helge was working as a farmhand outside Eslöv. After spending a few hours with a friend at a nearby farm, he was walking back home when he saw something utterly strange. He wasn't far from home when he saw, in the pale moonlight, a group of approximately a dozen men walking towards him. They weren't much taller than a meter from toe to the top of their heads and passed him so near that he could see their faces clearly. They had beards, some kind of hats, and were dressed in dark green clothes. Their faces were tough and cruel looking. "I became terribly frightened and had to force myself to not run away, he told Anders Liljegren. The group reminded him of marching soldiers, and he could hear them talk with each other but couldn't identify any words—despite that it was without a doubt some kind of language. They seemed aware of him, but still ignored his presence. After passing him, they turned out in a field and towards an intense white-blue light surrounded by fog—and they all disappeared into it. Soon the mysterious light followed them into the abyss with a swooshing sound. Helge noticed a strong, almost chemical smell that lingered in the area for a while afterward. "These weren't any normal humans; this was something from another world."

What kind of world, one might ask? An inner world, a projection of one's consciousness, some kind of gnome-like aliens? A dream? A misunderstanding? Maybe even a hoax? To be fair, I trust Helge. He seemed like a genuine man who was honestly perplexed over the incident. In later interviews, he claimed it was aliens, but in that first one, he had no idea what it was—but one thing is for sure, he knew what he saw, smelled, and heard.

Peter and Maria also met the unknown late one evening, seemingly from another world. Was the experience colored by Peter's interest in science fiction and UFOs, or a modern version of a gnome encounter? Maybe both? A projection of experiences and information towards something that otherwise would have been totally alien to the young witnesses.

In 2017, fifty years after the incident, UFO-Sverige managed to trace the now-adult witnesses. One of them, Maria, agreed to talk. Without presenting her with the information reported by the original investigator, Sven Schalin, in 1973, she drew a remarkably similar version of the creature she and Peter witnessed.

On the other hand, she had no memories of the eerie lights that led to their terrifying encounter. Maria added that a couple of weeks later she saw a white and red light shining through the window and that the family, on another occasion, heard weird noises down by the stream—like monkeys chattering.

It's important to note that Sven Schalin, a legend during his own time in the Swedish UFO community, was biased towards aliens. In his original investigation, he sees clues to alien humanoids and UFOs everywhere, which might have affected the teenagers and their families.

On the other hand, Maria revisiting the experience fifty years later with a new, very similar sketch of the creature is, after all, pretty sensational.

two
underground humanoids

THE DEPTH of the cave wasn't more than 15-20 meters and ended with a collapsed roof. "I highly doubt it's much deeper than the collapsed area," cave explorer Ingvar Borg said. There might have been disappointment in his voice. The local legends said the cave would be at least two hundred meters deep and lead to an extensive tunnel system. Down there, trolls and other mythical creatures roamed freely without the curious gaze of us mortal humans.

It was May 1974 when a team led by ufologist and cryptozoologist Jan-Ove Sundberg decided to take a closer look at the famous cave once and for all. He was joined by a bunch of merry men: Ingvar Borg, photographer Håkan Pettersson, ufologist and researcher Thorvald (later Bevan) Berthelsen, Ingvar Damm, and his father Bror Damm. Were the stories true? What would they find in there? Monsters? A gruesome death? Treasures? None of these things happened, but at least they had an answer: the cave wasn't especially deep and just led to a collapsed roof.

One tale told of a tunnel a few kilometers in length, leading all the way to another mountain, Nordboberget. It was said to be used by trolls to travel unnoticed by humans for hundreds of years. Now, crawling on their knees and bellies, the team of explorers soon understood it would be impossible for huge humanoids to use it as a pathway.

Contrary to popular belief, trolls in Scandinavian folklore aren't necessarily ugly, dumb, and scary. Just like in Richard Sharpe Shaver's story "I Remember Lemuria," with dim-witted Deros brutes and their counterparts in the beautiful and smart Teros, some trolls are tall, well-dressed, and downright dashing (dare I say sexy?) in looks and behavior. In many ways, they can be counted as shape-shifters, "dressing up" for the occasion. This often wasn't good for the humans who encountered them. Trolls can also take the shape of different kinds of animals, like cats and owls. To keep it simple, a troll is a form of physical/nonphysical shape-shifting nature spirit in Scandinavia. They could be small in stature and very well fit in the above-mentioned cave. Maybe it's time for a new expedition? Time will tell.

Humans have longed for the underworld throughout the history of mankind. From spiritual dwellings and fairy-tale stories to places of cave art and, of course, mining. The search for valuable metals has been with us as long as anyone can remember. All that glitters is gold in many ways—and the more difficult it is to find, the deeper we dig. The mining industry in Sweden goes back over a thousand years, and in total there have been over three thousand mines scattered throughout the country. The biggest export is still, to this day, iron ore.

The presence of mines has created many legends of apparitions one can meet down in the abyss if you're not careful. Or are they a co-creation between the cold, rocky depths and those who visit them? Would those liminal supernatural dwellers exist if it wasn't for the personality of the environments and the stories being told in relation to them?

The most widely spread character is Gruvfrun ("The Mine Lady"). Sometimes she's called Gruvrået, a very seductive entity, much like the forest version, Skogsrået.

Gruvfrun is often an omen for upcoming disasters and accidents down in the mines. If you see her, you should get to safety.

She also wants to be sure the mines are in good shape, and a sighting of her can mean that you need to clean up your mess. All kinds of animals (especially cats, dogs, goats, and such) found down in the mine belong to her and should never, ever be hurt or killed.

One can say that the constant search for what's underground and what one might meet down there is a physical manifestation of humans digging into their own subconsciousness. It's an eternal search for truth and enlightenment, from physical objects like buried treasures, minerals, and ore to the one thing we can't resist: mysteries. What we find in the abyss can also tell us about our shadow parts, the darkness in our hearts and minds. In the best case, we depart from the underground empty-handed or maybe with a treasure or lesson—or crushed to death by tons of rock.

There aren't many modern stories about underground humanoids in Sweden. However, there is one that attracted my attention. It first came to my knowledge just after coming home from a production in Malta. While there, I desperately tried to get tickets to visit the legendary underground temple and burial place of Hypogeum. I didn't succeed in getting inside, but finally back in Sweden, otherworldly creatures of a different, more home-grown kind met me. It was thanks to Rob Kristoffersen of the fine podcast *Our Strange Skies*.

"Hey, are you familiar with this case?" the message on Twitter said, accompanied by a short description of a very curious case. I was instantly hooked. "What the hell is this?" So I decided to dig deeper into this strange case.

It was the end of the summer of 1968 (or possibly 1969), in August, which for many Swedes is the ultimate part of the year, even if that means extreme heat combined with unexpected showers of rain. Oh, and the notion that it's soon all over, and months of relentless darkness await.

The time had just struck 3 p.m., and it was soon time for the kids, a group of boys between eleven and 13, to head back home.

As the impending doom of school was rushing closer each day, they probably decided on one last summer adventure.

They all came from Smedjebacken, an old mining and iron industry community with a couple of thousand inhabitants. The whole area is filled with old mines and other abandoned mining facilities. This wasn't the most famous mine in the area. That honor goes to the Flogberg mine, around ten kilometers north of their town. The word "flog" is an older word and is said to mean dragon fire, the light that was seen by people indicating that the ground was rich with ore and worth mining. And yes, there have always been tales about a dragon there, but that's a story for another book.

The boys had found an old root cellar near one of the mines and spent the day building a hut. Three of them, Benny Magnusson, Kjell Östling, and Staffan Helander, were on their way to join the other boys when they saw a very strange scene next to the mine entrance, not far from their hut.

The beings reacted to the presence of the boys, surprised by their sudden appearance. There were two of them, both identical and tall—up to 2.5 meters in height. "They looked like twins," Benny said in a later interview. They were dressed in white overalls and hoods that partly covered their human-looking faces. In later accounts of the incident, their faces are described slightly differently: the eyes on their long faces were bigger than usual, and their movements were swift and light, which felt—according to the boys—very "nonhuman." In their hands, they each had a white, briefcase-style bag. At a distance of approximately fifty meters, they were clearly visible to the surprised audience. The beings stopped and seemed to focus all their attention on them.

The boys suddenly felt paralyzed and couldn't move a muscle. After around five minutes, their frozen state went away, and they ran away in fear. The humanoids watched them for a moment and then started moving. Benny and the others ran on a path through the forest towards Highway 65 (now 66), and their new tall friends moved swiftly after them on the side of the path. One of the boys dropped his glasses during the escape, and Benny stopped to help him find them. "I looked up and made eye contact with them. They had piercing, big eyes, like they could look through me. And I really got a good look at how tall they were," he told me during a conversation much later. During this short time, the beings stopped and watched them in silence until Benny and his friend had worked up the courage to escape. It was the last adventure of the summer.

In an article from 1994, published in the homemade and not especially credible newsletter *Hårda Tider*, the description of the humanoids had become slightly different: The creatures were 230–240 cm tall and dressed in full-coverage white overalls with hoods. The head was round, and the face was gray-white with very large black eyes. The nose was narrow, long, and pointed, and the mouth was as small as a slit, without any visible lips. In Boris Jungqvist's book *Kontakt med UFO!*, the beings were described as slightly shorter, between 1.90 and 2 meters tall.

In my conversation with Benny, he told me something very interesting: the strangers floated a bit above the ground, and it seemed like they were moving in slow motion. Moving in slow motion is similar to what some of the children at the Ariel School incident in 1994 observed, a case Benny wasn't aware of when I mentioned it to him. The witnesses reported how the beings moved like they were in a different state of time, sometimes getting caught in a loop—repeating their movements over and over again. Could this be a distortion of time and space or just the reaction when the body and mind are being exposed to extreme stress and shock? A dear friend once told me how he, during a particularly stressful situation (he was the road manager for a band), suddenly experienced the world around him in extreme slow motion. The state lasted for about one hour, which, to be fair, made his part of the job easier.

There's no reason to question Benny's story; still, I'd like to explore a few alternatives. It could be a hoax, a prank from a gang of boys who are late to dinner. It wouldn't be the first or the last time, as children will be children. They are armed with an overactive imagination and have difficulties separating our traditional consensus reality from fairy tales. A prank that got out of hand and became a "real" experience to the boys, is by all means a reality by itself. Mats Nilsson, a *UFO-Sverige* veteran, once told me: *"an inner experience could be as real as an outer experience."* And I tend to agree. In a child's world, especially with peer pressure, anything can happen.

It's a tricky situation, as none of us knows what happened that afternoon, and the information is sparse. I had no reason to disbelieve Benny, a kind and honest man, when listening to his matter-of-fact account of the events. He actually brought down the strangeness a few notches in comparison to what had been written years later. Maybe I'm naive, but in this case, it makes it more credible. Bear in mind that I feel that famous incidents, such as the above-mentioned Ariel School in Ruwa, Zimbabwe, the Broad Haven Primary school in Pembrokeshire, Wales, and Westall High School in Melbourne, Australia, all ring true—and all of them involve larger groups of children observing out-of-this-world events. I can buy the concept of mass hysteria to a certain point, but sooner or later, some of those involved must start to doubt the experience—or feel bad for agreeing with the others just for the sake of belonging. Peer pressure and all that.

It should be noted that only Benny, Kjell, and Staffan claim to remember this whole event—the other boys have no memory whatsoever of it. When I mentioned the Smedjebacken humanoid case to my friend and podcast co-host Jimmy Beris, he had another theory that is worth bringing up: moonshining.

The county of Dalarna has been notorious for its moonshining industry for a long time. Maybe not as much today as in the past, considering it's cheap nowadays to import (and sometimes smuggle) booze.

It was a different time in 1968. Finding a good location for brewing was always a priority. Imagine setting up the equipment in an abandoned mine where no one dares to go inside. One day, dressed in protective clothing and helmets, you find a group of kids outside. What would you do? One thing is to freak them out by staring at them and then run after them when they flee for their lives. Even though it wasn't the original purpose of the scare, the rest of the story is up to the vivid imagination of the children. An encounter with moonshiners is transformed into a meeting with creepy big-eyed humanoids from the darkest depths!

It's up for debate, like with all the cases in this book, what really happened. Maybe it's not important? I feel that what really matters is how it affected the witnesses afterward. What did the experience give them—or take away?

Benny told me how the humanoid encounter began a lifelong passion for UFOs and aliens. He has seen hundreds of them over the years, mostly in the shape of golden discs. Earthly artifacts like golden discs are said in many cultures to represent higher deities. Somehow I think that the observation of UFOs can represent the same thing. And like with all deities, it's up to those meeting them to use the experience in whatever way it matters to them. Did this incident trigger something in Benny—either a very vivid imagination or just the possibility to look beyond the veil of reality? Did the humanoids offer him a key to the unknown?

In my essay "High Strangeness, the Oz Factor, and Symbols," I wrote: "During the Ariel school incident, the children were bombarded by images of the world, and through that, learned that we need to take care of it. Symbols, such as images, make us learn faster and more effectively, and it's way more fun than reading long, boring manuals on how to behave. What if it all, both UFOs and their inhabitants, are symbols at work? A sighting of a UFO or a being makes us think, as it's so absurd and unreal and beyond our reality. If the phenomenon is a language by itself, everything might seem absurd at first. Remember that a foreign language is nonsense until you've learned it."

Jacques Vallée goes into similar territory in his book *Dimensions*: "Emerging fully armed into our local universe, the UFOs provide the physical support for our own dreams. We do the rest.

Our brains erect a ladder of symbols toward the darkened skies where the strange machines hover, and we meet them more than halfway across the bridge of their strangeness—perhaps because we vaguely perceive that their irresistible, pathetic adventure is closely related to our own. But the extraterrestrial theory is not good enough, because it is not strange enough to explain the facts."

David J. Moore explores the concept of UFOs as archetypes and metaphors in his 2019 philosophical exploration of the phenomenon, *Evolutionary Metaphors*, and comes to the conclusion: "The phenomenon itself seems to be attempting to teach us something about our reality, and it certainly benefits us to know precisely what that might be. The UFO, like the occult, becomes a poignant symbol of inner transformation, and rather than simply being a field of inner knowledge of the unseen, the UFO appears to be an entirely seen phenomenon, and seems to infer another realm of Being and beings."

Some witness testimonies might sound bizarre; however, it could be because they—and we—are desperately trying to make sense of the unknown. The brain looks for patterns, and those patterns can take very mysterious paths. Mines and caves are, in many ways, manifestations of our own curiosity, of exploring the unknown, of traveling where no person has gone before.

Where there is space to explore, both internally and externally, humanity will venture. Just imagine whom or what we might encounter when carving out those paths, whether in space, on land, or underground.

three **boxes**

THERE IS something special about the vast landscapes outside of crowded cities, where life—allegedly—is calmer and more down-to-earth, grounded so to speak. The long potholed roads surrounded by endless forests make us contemplate existence. It might be difficult to avoid, as the landscape reveals itself in front of us whether we like it or not, exposed to its rugged beauty.

In places where there is silence, there is time to empty the mind and stop the endless circles of thought. Instead, we're opening up doors into the void and letting ourselves explore our consciousness and feelings, all those things that are beyond thought. It's deeper than thoughts, maybe profound. The lack of distortions in nature is considered by many to be the true form of existence. Its chaotic entity embraces us, instead of us embracing it.

In the Örnsköldsvik commune, located over an hour away by car from the city with the same name, lies the small village of Trehörningsjö, which literally means "Triangle Lake" or "a lake with three corners." The village is situated at the edge of an oddly shaped body of water, more akin to a twisted, crooked cross than a triangle, which connects via a stream to the two largest lakes in the area: Inre Lemesjön and Yttre Lemesjön.

Like many small communities in the north of Sweden, Trehörningsjö's existence once depended largely on the forest industry and farming. However, over the years, like many other places, it has been severely depopulated. Not that it was ever a big community to begin with; at the time of the story we're delving into, the population hadn't even reached 400, and today it's dwindled to less than 150 souls.

It's a place where time moves at a different speed, far from what you'll ever experience in our main capital, Stockholm, or other big cities like Göteborg and Malmö. And maybe it's that feeling of seclusion, distance, that makes it one of the most interesting hotspots for UFO activity in Sweden?

In 1969, the skies were less crammed with satellites, airplanes, and pollution. Under one of those evening skies, Kjell Näslund, part-time manager for the transmitter station at Hemliden, had an incredibly strange experience. The station is located just two kilometers outside the village, and it was there that he saw something truly out of the ordinary on March 12 of that year. He kept quiet for three years, as his story was met with suspicion and mockery at the time of the incident. Kjell finally shared his experience with researcher Ragnar Söderberg in 1972.

It was around 6 p.m. when Kjell arrived at the station. It was a cold evening, between minus 20 to 25 degrees Celsius, and the sky was clear. As he had done many times before, he did a routine check of the equipment and then sat down in the small kitchenette to read the evening newspaper. It didn't take long until his peace was disturbed by the sound of alarms, one after another. The transmitter station, which helped send out television and radio signals, indicated severe interference. As both the phone, radio, and television worked, he was surprised to see that every indicator lamp was glowing red.

Scratching his head, he took a look outside, but nothing was to be seen. The next step was to call his colleagues at the transmitter station in Sundsvall to tell them about the situation. Eventually, the alarms stopped, and the lamps went dark. Kjell had no idea what was going to happen soon after.

At Approximately at 6:30 pm., half an hour after arriving at his workplace, he suddenly had a feeling. "It was like something told me to go outside, like an impulse coming to me! When he opened the door and looked out, he saw something that would forever change his life, and it was about to get even stranger.

Fifteen meters away from the door where he was standing, a deforested area began and continued down a depression. An enormous craft was hovering ominously right outside. It was at the same level as the facility, which was constructed on higher ground. With a diameter of 150 meters and a height of about five to six meters, the craft completely covered the depression all around the station. The contours of it were slightly undefined and fuzzy. Kjell couldn't, understandably, believe his eyes. The experience didn't become less strange when he noticed the opening. "It was like a three-dimensional film, a tunnel into the craft." It had a gray-blue glow coming from the entrance, and there was movement both inside and outside. Some kind of intelligent beings were present.

"They were like spray-painted boxes, like clouds without clearly defined edges. They levitated about two inches above the ground and were about 130 to 135 centimeters tall with a width of 30 to 40 centimeters." Kjell saw around ten beings, three or four of them inside the strange tunnel, the rest outside. In a later interview, he was asked if he thought the scene could have been a film projection of some sort, but he dismissed that idea. It was simply too odd to properly be described in words.

While studying the strangeness unfolding in front of him, the thought struck him that maybe he should call the police—not just because it was an unexplainable event he was witnessing, but also because the station was most probably a protected area. This was in 1969, in the middle of the Cold War. Russia wasn't far away, and Sweden was constantly on high alert, even with its traditional so-called neutral stance during international conflicts.

Once again, a feeling stopped him from leaving his position to pick up the phone. Instead, he felt an urge to let them inside.

Holding up the door, he saw how seven or eight "boxes" floated inside, just centimeters away from him. Our stunned transmitter station manager wanted to reach out and touch them, and once again he couldn't move. It felt like someone communicated telepathically what he should do or not do. It was here, while studying the visitors up close, he sensed that their appearance was some kind of shell, like a protection. On the inside, there was something else, not necessarily a physical body. Maybe some kind of intelligence? This, whatever it was, told him that he should keep calm and that they weren't dangerous.

The shells, just like the craft itself, were shivering, vibrating—like air during a scorching hot summer day. He couldn't smell any odor or hear any sound except buzzing from the transmitter station itself. Slowly, "at the same speed as a human walking calmly," the boxes entered the station and seemed to inspect the interior and equipment. After five to ten minutes, they went back to their craft and, for lack of better words, got sucked into the tunnel. The craft then went off in a northern direction and disappeared into the cold of the night.

Kjell could move freely again and went directly back to the kitchen to call his friend Hans Häggblad, a local police officer. Hans took down his statement, but after inspecting the view from where he was living, nothing was to be seen over Hemliden. When Kjell called his colleagues in Sundsvall, they laughed at him and asked if he was drunk. His wife didn't take him too seriously either. "I want to say that I was sober and balanced, and fully awake. I have no explanation for this. It is what it is," he later added in an interview for *UFO-Information*, 1972.

What happened to Kjell that evening? Looking at it now, there's a dreamlike feeling over the event. From the box-like and slightly cloudy, undefined entities to the enormous UFO with similar properties.

Did Kjell fall asleep in the kitchenette and dream about everything? Kjell was considered a very reliable, practical man, someone who could separate fact from fiction—so in his mind, this happened as he witnessed it.

The repeated telephone calls, first to his friend the policeman and then to his colleagues in Sundsvall, might hint that the whole event did happen in an awake state of mind. Kjell being the only witness to this event makes it less believable, so why did he even tell people about his experience? Wouldn't it be easier to let it go, or at least blame it on a dream? Let's, for once, set aside the idea that everyone wants attention, which just isn't true. Kjell didn't make any money from it. He didn't seem to be the kind of man who wanted to have his life invaded by UFO researchers and hear how his neighbors and colleagues laughed behind his back.

I'm not saying this experience belongs to our shared objective reality—a tangible event with undisputed proof.

Let's jump ahead in time to 1977—the year yours truly was born, Elvis died, and Kurt Nilsson experienced something very similar at the exact same spotyct slightly different. Kurt, a -year-old shortwave radio amateur, took his car one evening at 6:30 p.m. and drove around to test out his equipment mounted in his vehicle. While in Trehörningsjö, he noticed that the quality of the broadcasting was lacking and decided to go farther up to Hemliden, the transmitter station. He wanted to avoid the interference on lower ground. He was in radio contact with a friend in Domsjö, and when getting closer to the station, the interference became even more intense. At the top, just beside the main antenna, they ended the conversation. Usually, according to Kurt, when the quality was bad, both of them would hear the same interference. This time Kurt heard his friend clearly; however, his broadcasting quality was severely lacking.

Alone up there, still in his car, he looked around and noticed a bright blue light from slightly below him, down in a depression (not stated if this was the same depression where Kjell saw his craft). In front of a small hill, something was visible.

At first, he didn't take much interest in it, yet the longer he observed the scene, the more strange it became: "It was some kind of machine, with a dome on the top and a few meters in diameter. In front of it stood three figures, dressed in space-overalls." Kurt was around one hundred meters away and could clearly see the shapes of the beings, dressed in grayish overalls and approximately sixty centimeters tall. They had tightly fit gloves and "space helmets," similar to what astronauts had at the time, with a big opening in the front for better sight. The craft seemed to be hovering above the ground.

Still a bit perplexed by what he saw, he turned on the car lights. At the same moment the lights came on, the odd view in front of him disappeared! Where the craft and the beings stood moments before, it was now empty. He turned off the lights, and the craft and the silhouettes of the beings appeared once again. As the situation had turned from weird to plain creepy, Kurt did what many others would do: he started the car and decided to get the hell away from there!

He was scared out of his mind but didn't get far. Just fifty meters down the road from the station, he had to stop, as the beings, all three of them, were standing in the middle of the road blocking his path!

The one in the middle held an object shaped like a small spade. As the being made a movement with the object, the lights and motor of Kurt's car were turned off.

"This is it!" he thought, but somehow kept calm and waited a few seconds. He started the motor, put the car in reverse, and backed up ten meters. He sat there in silence for a few minutes and then, once again, turned on the lights. The trio of visitors was gone, and he drove away as fast as he could down the dark, murky road. Kurt was considered a trustworthy man, someone who wasn't eager to make up things for the sake of attention. Just like Kjell. It didn't take long for investigators to arrive, and a few days later, they examined the spot and found that someone had taken samples of the moss and soil. There were also footprints, child-sized footprints.

While I respect Kurt's experience, it just doesn't sound right to me. I don't want to be a boring skeptic here; maybe Kurt really saw something—it just wasn't what he thought it was. Maybe what he saw was a car, a so-called EPA-traktor. These vehicles are rebuilt cars, originally used as buses or farm machines. During later years, they became popular for teenagers to cruise around with, as they aren't allowed to go over a certain speed limit. Let's say that three teenagers parked their car on the field, slacking off and doing nothing, as teenagers do. They were dressed in warm clothes and maybe helmets. This was on October 18, and the snow must have covered the landscape by then. Maybe it was a snowmobile instead of a car, and the distance of one hundred meters, in combination with the strong light from the machine, made it look otherworldly. The teenagers, probably scared themselves, decided to run off over the road, where they met Kurt and his car.

Could it be that his perception was tinted by Kjell's story? The mind can be a suggestive devil.

It should be noted that no traces of a car or any other machine were found at the spot of the alleged landing. There was a scratch mark on a tree almost three meters above the ground and signs of someone - or something disturbing the moss. This is in comparison to the 1969 incident, where three trees were found cut at the top, all at a height of 15 meters.

Personally, I find the "aliens" in the 1969 incident to be of high interest; they're so different from many other witness reports. Are there any similar incidents in Sweden with box-shaped creatures? You bet.

Ragnar Söderberg, the investigator who first interviewed Kjell in 1972, found another interesting incident from January 1959. From his home in Dombäck, sixty-two-year-old Gottfrid Olsson looked out the window and saw a strange red-white glowing (with a blue line in the middle) entity on the other side of the road. It was the size of a normal human being, though from the shoulders down—including the legs—it had a box-like appearance, with sharp edges and straight lines. The head was more blurry and undefined. The being/object stood still for three to four minutes and then disappeared in a sudden flash.

Another similar incident, observed during the night of August 31, 1981, was told by an anonymous witness to taxi driver Arne Lundberg. He reported it to UFO-Sverige and their magazine *UFO-Aktuellt* in 1985. The witness, called EV, was on her way home in Haverdal, north of Halmstad (along the Kattegat sea, bordering on Denmark), when she suddenly felt like she was walking into an invisible wall. Not being able to move, she saw what looked like a luminous white human shape with a defined head and shoulders connected down to a rectangular body. It was leaning towards the fence of her house, at least that's what it looked like to her.

She tried to talk to it, believing at first it was her boyfriend, but the shape didn't respond or move. When she finally was able to move, the mysterious shape was gone.

Is it, as I mentioned earlier, the presence of the infinite void of silence that opens up to experiences like this? The sense of being alone in the universe that comes while spending a lot of time in environments like this? Your mind wanders, daydreams appear, and suddenly you've entered another realm of reality. Maybe that happened to Kjell, maybe not. Is this one of those events when you wake up and think that everything is true and immediately tell your friends, and then realize that it was a dream, and still stick to the story just to keep your prestige?

Sometimes it might be better to keep telling a story about aliens than admitting to not being able to separate dreams from reality.

Once I lay in my bed, probably fell asleep and woke up again believing I had committed a double murder in my mom's old office. I had buried the bodies and their motorcycles in a field and then gotten away with it. Sitting on the bed trying to figure out how much this would change my life—it would destroy everything I had built up so far! The sense of impending doom was so strong! It took me twenty to thirty minutes to fully understand this was just a dream. I didn't stay in that illusion for long and have told the story many times as an example of how dreams can affect you—but in the end, it's still just what it is, a dream.

In Kjell's case, it feels like it would have been easier to admit it was only a dream instead of continuing to tell the same story year after year about box-shaped, cloudy beings inspecting his workplace and then leaving in their humongous, oversized craft.

Kjell was practical and down-to-earth and far from being into woo and making up things. He shared his work at the transmitter station with his job as a driver. He was a respected and passionate enthusiast for all things regarding local culture and outdoor life, and he was known to be trusted.

The incident still lives on as a mystery and has been analyzed and discussed countless times among UFO researchers. No one has come up with a logical, rational explanation. It's one of those stories that stays with you.

four
frogmen in black

I COULD ALMOST SENSE HIM, the man behind me. Well, first, I saw him—he was passing me in the opposite direction—and there was a slight delay in his movements, like he was checking me out. Not in a flirtatious way, more like surveillance. I was walking up from the store to my apartment, not expecting anything out of the ordinary. But the notion of the phenomenon Men in Black, from now on called MiB, was on my mind at the moment. When I turned around, feeling his eyes burning on my neck, I saw him standing in the middle of the pavement, looking up at me. "Better to ignore," I thought and continued up to the left, over the street and among the tall pines facing the apartment house. For some reason, I looked behind me again, and there he stood on the path covered with pine needles. The mysterious man wore a jacket with a hoodie, covering his face with shadows. He stood there frozen, watching me, which gave me chills, and I hurried inside and locked the door behind me.

Later that day, I was joking with my partner about how a MiB was following me. This was mostly because it was something I was researching at the time, and I was told not to worry. A while later, I was home alone when I noticed how the cats were reacting to something in the hallway. They were focusing their attention on the door. To my horror, I could see the doorknob moving slowly, as if someone was trying to get inside, similar to the scene in John Carpenter's *The Thing* when a deep-frozen Kurt Russell comes back to the base and finds himself locked out. Through the twisted peephole perspective, I saw a man standing there, as if he was waiting for me to open the door. And I did, contrary to common sense. "“Are you looking for someone?” I asked. He answered with one word: “Loam.” I explained to him, both nervous and annoyed, that there was no “Loam” in this apartment and said goodbye. He hung around outside the door for a while and then left.

This was the start of more than a month of strange visits. Once, he rang the doorbell in the middle of the night, asking the same question. Another time, standing outside on the balcony, we found him looking up at us. At first, we could only see his white eyes, which were almost luminous in the dark evening. It became routine, and we would find him outside our door or on the floor above, repeatedly looking down at our apartment. And he always asked the same question: “Loam?”

Much later, long after he disappeared, I looked up Loam in Allen H. Greenfield's book *The Secret Cipher of the Ufonauts*, a cipher allegedly found in Aleister Crowley's *Book of the Law*. I became more obsessed with it because it reminded me of the names old-school contactees usually came up with when talking about the strange otherworldly beings they claimed to be in contact with, such as Ashtar, Orthon, Semjase, Aura Rhanes, and many others. Typing in “Loam” in the cipher revealed sinister words like “soul,” “crawl,” and “shadows” appearing, and that didn't help my paranoia. Loam itself is a form of soil made from three forms of soil: sand, silt, and clay. It can also be spelled “Lam, which comes from old English, Lām (clay, mud, mire, earth). Lam also happens to be the alleged alien entity that Aleister Crowley channeled during his 1908 Amalantrah workings, which became even more famous for the eerie portrait Crowley drew of it, a large-headed, gray-like character.

So what the heck is all of this? Beats me, but one thing the MiB phenomenon leads to is paranoia. It seems to be the perfect pathway to that dreaded rabbit hole of conspiracies and high strangeness, something countless (maybe all) witnesses have experienced ever since Gray Barker wrote about Albert K. Bender's encounters in the 1956 classic *They Knew Too Much About Flying Saucers*, and later, Bender himself in 1962's *Flying Saucers and the Three Men*.

Even though I had read about them earlier in various UFO literature at my local library as a kid, the MiB phenomenon did not truly capture my attention until the release of Barry Sonnenfeld's blockbuster *Men in Black* (1997). The movie portrayed the elusive so-called MiBs as the saviors of the universe and all-around good guys from a hero's viewpoint—despite their disturbing tendency to erase people's memories from time to time with a literal flash. It's a great popcorn movie, and I must admit that it combines action, comedy, and mystery perfectly. The details incorporated in the movie were something that only a twenty-year-old guy with an interest in the unknown would know, which made it even more exciting.

I've been intrigued for a long time to find out if there are any observations of MiB in Sweden, which turned into a hard nut to crack and a lot of digging. To be fair, there's not much to go on when it comes to this subject here, and the few stories that exist are things one should take with a grain of salt. I'd still like to share a few of them with you—no matter the credibility of those making the reports.

Jan-Ove Sundberg was a journalist, ufologist, and cryptozoologist (who had a short stint of fame with his *GUST* – Global Underwater Search Team, between 1997 and 2001), and whose name shows up from time to time in the annals of high strangeness. Sundberg, who was considered highly unreliable, relayed several stories involving MiB from his research, but it should be noted he was also a notorious hoaxer, compulsive liar, stalker, and many other—even more horrifying—things. One day I'll dig deeper into his strange and disturbing life, but let's focus on the stories he told for now, for example, the one about Loch Ness.

On the morning of August 16, 1971, cherub-faced Sundberg was in Foyers Bay, located in the middle of the famous lake, stumbling around in the wild, trying to get to the construction site of a power station. He was working on a story about the Loch Ness monster for the gentleman's magazine *Lektyr*. Whatever he was looking for in the bushes didn't prepare him for the sight he saw moments later. In front of him, in an open space among the trees, stood a strange craft (which reminded him, or maybe more the staff at *Flying Saucer Review*, of a giant smoothing iron, more specifically a classic Husqvarna. The similarity is striking). Outside of it appeared, from the bushes, three alleged aliens, all dressed in what looked like gray diver's suits (this is a theme that will come back in Sundberg's own mythology of the MiB. More on that later). The beings climbed aboard the craft and flew silently away and seemed to descend again at Loch Mhor. This is the short version, in a story that's been thoroughly investigated by, for example, FSR and Stuart Campbell in 1981 (in a follow-up article to the 1973 original report by Ted Holiday) who concluded that the whole thing was totally made up by Sundberg.

Anyway, when he came back to his hometown of Motala, Sweden, mysterious MiB visited him at his house, and anonymous callers told him to keep quiet about the incident. Another time, a black figure walked around in his garden during the night, leaving strange, dumbbell-shaped footprints. He also suffered from poltergeist phenomena and disturbing dreams. Sensationally enough, he claimed to have photographs of the strange-looking UFO, but not a single photo appeared—at least not one that actually showed something tangible. Sundberg claimed to have sent photographic evidence to Dr. James Harder at APRO, but nothing more is known about this. One might think that Sundberg, after telling his remarkable story, just didn't want to comment further to any curious investigators, for the sole reason he was bluffing.

When confronted with the discrepancies raised by FSR in 1981 via the *AFU Newsletter*'s Anders Liljegren, Sundberg's initial reaction was hesitant: "What can I say to make people believe me? I have seen what I have seen!" He then declared that he had decided to withdraw somewhat from the ufology scene for his own good: "I've never felt as good in my life as I do now. I have discovered it's important to keep a certain distance from the subject and not be too involved." He also mentioned in his communication with researchers and investigators that the entire experience with the drama involving the UFO and the mysterious men resulted in a nervous breakdown, so he didn't feel like bringing it up again. In his articles about his investigation of Loch Ness, he never mentioned seeing a UFO or aliens. The whole matter appeared to be a sensitive subject for him. I will leave Jan-Ove Sundberg for now, but I will return to him shortly for some additional MiB observations, whether true or not. Instead, let's examine a beloved and trustworthy man.

Bevan Berthelsen was, during a couple of hectic years in the 1970s, one of the most active proponents of the UFO subject in Sweden, including being the chairman of UFO-Sverige between 1976 and 1978. However, his interest actually started as early as the summer of 1972. At the time, Bevan, who hadn't changed his name from Thorvald yet, considered UFOs and aliens to be a laughing matter. He didn't take it seriously at all! This night would change it all because of a good old case of sleepwalking. He left his bed, got dressed, and took his bike (sleep-cycling?) around two kilometers to the desolate area of Slätängen, where he found himself awake and wondering what the heck he was doing there in the middle of the night. Oddly enough, he plucked a bouquet of bluebells before cycling home again, confused over his first and only encounter with the gentle art of sleepwalking.

One week later, he noticed how he got the urge to read and study everything about the UFO subject and borrowed all the books he could find at the library. This led him to start *Köpings UFO-förening* in January 1973, and not long after, on March 11 of the same year, he and three other witnesses saw a cylinder-shaped object passing over his hometown, Köping. It was the start of an obsession that lasted until 1980 when he left the UFO community and joined the spiritual movement Subud together with his wife.

But what about those mysterious MiB? Well, the same day his UFO observation hit the local newspaper, he heard a knock on the door. Living in a country house with views in all directions, the visitor seemed to have appeared from nowhere. Knocking on the door was a man in his thirties, dressed in a brown suit and white shirt, with suntanned skin and slanted eyes—but not, as Bevan could see, of Asian descent.

"How are you feeling?" the man said, asking for directions. After receiving instructions on how to continue down the road, he left the head-scratching owner. "Who the hell was that?" Bevan thought and ran out, looking for him—but the odd-looking man was gone. The road went straight in both directions, with no places for the man to hide.

This might not seem overly strange, but remember, this is the countryside in Sweden in 1973, and it was a very "exotic" experience at the time. Bevan felt that this was truly something out of the ordinary. As a comparison, I can mention how my mother, in her youth, dyed her hair black and directly received aggressive and racist reactions from other Swedes. So the sight of someone not looking typically Swedish was something rare. This could, of course, also count for Bevan's own reaction; the man with his slanted eyes felt out of place.

In 1993, Jan-Ove Sundberg, who was, in all fairness, a quite good writer, published his second book, *Fantomubåtarna* (*The Phantom Submarines*), where he claimed that the years of submarine encounters in the archipelago along the Scandinavian coasts really were USOs, unidentified submerged objects—basically, aquatic aliens. What's true or not in this book is difficult to say, but there's a big chance that a lot of it was based on actual observations—but with a lot of added (and retracted) details from

Sundberg's side. However, there are a few interesting MiB-style encounters that are worth bringing up. Just take them with a grain of salt—sea salt at least—as we're talking about something as strange as... FROGMEN IN BLACK!

One witness, Torbjörn Danielsson, had his encounter in 1982. He was working at a sawmill when a SAAB 900 EMS drove up beside him outside the mill. The driver gesticulated, and Torbjörn understood that he wanted to say something. Beside him in the passenger seat was another man, both of whom had slightly dark skin and tailored suits. "They had angular faces, almost like they were chiseled. They looked like brothers." He compared them to stick figures because of their very plain looks. They also spoke an unusually "pure" Swedish with no dialects and sounded like they were reading the news. The man asked several odd questions, including "What's your time cycle?" (a weird detail that coincides with an episode of *The Haunted Objects* podcast I listened to at the time of writing this). A while later, he saw them down by the water, together with a third man dressed in diver's suits. Some would say foreign spies, but in Sundberg's opinion, these were clearly MiBs.

On the evening of October 18, 1989, a witness (out fishing) observed an object in the water, similar to a submarine, surrounded by eight to ten frogmen. They were shorter than usual, around 150–160 centimeters in length, dressed in black diver's suits, some kind of transparent protection in front of their faces, and neither—that he could see—had any kind of diving equipment.

Two years later, on November 7, 1990, a man was out walking his collie and met four frogmen coming up from the water. They stared at him, causing him to feel a terrible fear! "I don't know how the thought struck me, but they didn't seem to be totally human. Their piercing eyes kind of hypnotized me, and I got paralyzed and unable to get away from there!" The frogmen walked past him, two on each side, and a few hundred meters away the paralysis stopped. He could see how they went into the water and disappeared. In total, Sundberg recounts twenty-six encounters with mysterious frogmen, often with—in the case their skin was visible - a darker complexion, no visible equipment, and in most cases caused both irrational and rational fear in the witnesses. In several cases, the witnesses received weird or threatening phone calls afterward, and in one case, the collie-man from 1990, he found prints of frogman shoes outside his house.

Now, once again, take these reports with a huge grain of sea salt, considering the source of them, the infamous Jan-Ove Sundberg. In an interview in *Sökaren*, 1984, he said without shame, "I actually think people in this country want to read lies, scams, and fraud! They read it as a form of entertainment." Jan-Ove passed away in 2011, years old, from cancer, after learning he would live to the tender age of 83 from a famous astrologer in New Delhi. He's still talked about today in Swedish ufology, but not because of all the good he did - —instead, it's actually the opposite. There's no question, though, how his legacy will forever be cemented into the world of high strangeness.

No matter what, the MiB phenomenon is fascinating, both as personal experiences and as mythology within ufology. These nicely dressed characters feel like they're coming from folklore, connected to fairy tales and legends. Their smooth appearances and odd behavior isn't far from the old trolls and fairies of Swedish folklore, symbols of both danger and adventure. Maybe they're sprung from biblical mythology and the three wise men/kings, most likely meant to be magicians: Caspar, Melchior, and Balthazar. Like so many modern MiBs, they show up during and after strange lights in the sky and end up doing some unauthorized stalking. Maybe that story is the start of the mythology we've learned to love and fear so much, or is there something more to it than biblical memes? Let's speculate a bit, or at least, let me do it. I'm going to take one for the team, so please follow me into the wilderness of speculative ramblings.

In an earlier text published on Medium, titled "Memes in Black," I explored the concept of Men in Black as symbols and wrote down the following—and highly speculative—hypotheses on what they might be.

Imperfections in an Artificial Reality

According to a popular fringe hypothesis, we are living in a simulated reality. This nonmaterial universe is controlled by someone or something, either programming us to behave in a certain way or letting us roam free in a test environment for some kind of experiment. Personally, I believe that if this is true, we are living in an organic simulation, the result of oozing slime on top of a pulsating, intergalactic mushroom on some distant, far-off planet. But that's a different story, and please don't take it too seriously.

Let's imagine that our reality is artificial, like the game *The Sims*, but so advanced that we wouldn't even notice when it's created in front of us, depending on where we look or how we behave. However, even with technology millions of years more advanced than ours, it wouldn't be perfect. Perfection is never perfect; there's always something "wrong," something "off," especially when it comes to intelligent beings.

For example, if dolphins are such godlike creatures, why would they want to mate with a human diver? Wouldn't they be intelligent enough to understand that the diver is of a different species or that it's plain wrong to have sex with someone who's not interested in such amorous activities? Intelligence doesn't necessarily mean being smart, you know.

Moreover, what if the MiBs are viruses intruding in our existence, trying to interfere with our daily lives, especially if we've encountered any kinds of anomalies in programming, bugs, or the paranormal? Their behavior would not be able to replicate our own perfectly, and their way of talking, thinking, and moving would be slightly different and, in some cases, extremely different from ours. Their often darker skin color could be connected to the racist idea that humans with darker skin are less trustworthy, something that's more evident than ever now in this chaotic existence, and that makes us see the MiBs as such.

Surveillance and Communication

UFOs have been seen for hundreds, maybe thousands, of years. They've gone through several incarnations, like chariots from the gods, airships, campy '50s flying saucers, spheres, and eggs, even rockets, and nowadays more and more complex geometrical shapes—truly otherworldly compared to our understanding of reality. I mean, who the heck flies a plain, metallic-looking cube? Or one with a sphere within it? An alien race might! Outside the abduction culture, there haven't been that many sightings of actual aliens either, except gray figures of short stature, the infamous Nazi-tinted "Nordics" (blond, tall Christ-wannabes), hairy dwarves, a couple of giants, maybe a mantis or two, and similar beings with humanoid features: one head, two arms, and legs. To be honest, if there are intelligent civilizations out there—how big a chance is it that they would be even the slightest similar to how humans are built? Maybe they're so damn weird they either let us see them as something less disturbing—or maybe they even never set their feet on this planet and instead send in humanlike probes that mimic our behavior, looks, and way of thinking—but as the extraterrestrials (or ultraterrestrials) themselves are way too different from us, they can only guess how a human would work, and the result is weird-looking men in old-fashioned clothes and cars behaving unnaturally. A good example is Guillermo del Toro's *Mimic* (1997), where cockroaches imitate humans to get close to us (and eat us, but let's not think about that). Like astronauts dressed as humans, these aliens take a closer look at those of us who might have noticed them and let them know, in a very awkward manner, that we should stay away and mind our own business. Maybe they're not even organic, just robotic reproductions of what might look like a human? The way we and they communicate is too abstract, so they send in something to maybe

—just maybe—get a chance to understand what's going on. Which might explain the unnatural, robotic behavior in some MiB observations.

Collective Creations

In some ways, maybe this is the wildest, most far-fetched hypothesis, as it deals with the nonmaterial, the esoteric, and the occult: the MiBs are created by our own collective consciousness as a way to find order in a world of chaos and explanations for the high strangeness around us. I've always felt that we get what we deserve, and through our collective consciousness, we unwittingly create figures that are harmful to our world. I believe that we, to a certain degree, create material entities without our intention to do so. This is not as crazy as it sounds, but more like this: every dictator/destructive person of power is a collective creation taken from millions upon millions of humans and the darker parts of their minds. Imagine all that small-minded bitterness, all that racism and greed that never fully develops into something more serious but slowly grows subconsciously inside us all, leaking out in small doses from us all and just grows bigger as it finds like-minded feelings. All hate and greed and stupidity are slowly creating a race of hateful people, some more and some less, which creates a society of stupidity—shaping newer generations, from parents to kids to friends to co-workers to... you get my point. Maybe the MiBs are tulpas, created from our own imagination into a material manifestation, and now we can't get rid of them. Watch Jane Schoenbrun's archive documentary, *A Self-Induced Hallucination* (2018), for a closer and excellent look at this abstract yet so tangible concept, the shape of Slenderman.

There is very little evidence—as with much in this field—of the existence of the MiB. I suggest we need to look at the phenomenon as something purely esoteric, a manifestation of some sort. Not necessarily like tulpas or similar thought-manifestations, but as symbolic projections of our own paranoia.

When experiencing something out of the ordinary, our senses sharpen and go into high alert, and things that are usually ordinary, or at least a little bit odd, get excessively exaggerated. The looks the mailman gives you become more intense, and facial features turn more extreme. We start to see details we never noticed before. One example is Viveca, who, together with her friend, met a tall man ("the tallest man I've ever seen!") dressed in a dark suit at a nightclub. He acted weird and awkward and wore old-fashioned glasses, like something from the sixties. He went up to her, bowed, and disappeared into the night again. The next day, Viveca was out walking her dog when he once again appeared, bowed to her, and continued to walk. She noticed his hair was pitch black and didn't move at all, like it was glued to his head. In the eyes of Viveca, she had just met the archangel Michael! It's all in the eyes of the beholder, as the old saying goes.

Another very bizarre incident happened to the Swedish psychic medium and witch Serafia Andersson during a session in a solarium. From her angle, she could look out into the room around the equipment and suddenly saw a tall man dressed in black in the corner of the room. Moments later, he was much closer, looking in at her and saying, "We can't do this where I come from," and then disappeared. A typical example of the absurd humor the phenomenon often exhibits. An interesting detail here is that if one looks back at the bizarre abduction (though he went quite willingly, at least with a mysterious pill) of Carl Higdon on October 25, 1974, the alien he claimed to have met said, "Your sun burns us." What is it with alleged visitors from outer space/another realm and not being able to do some serious sun tanning?

I'm not denying mysterious visits can come from military personnel, three-letter agencies, or other kinds of spooks—it's something that might be very likely when it comes to stuff that's been reported as unusual and comes to the government's knowledge, but I'd say that the concept of MiB is projected onto these incidents, making them seem stranger than they really are.

This can be very much rooted in our nature to keep our guards up—but also, if you allow me to go even more wild, a projection of the phenomenon (as in something paraweird, nonmaterial) onto other human beings around us. For a moment, minutes, hours, or days, it uses the human symbols around us as proxies for something extraordinary and sometimes even scary.

People can be unwilling actors, without their knowledge, in our own event-riddled universe. Like avatars for the unknown.

Let's end this with a fascinating little experience as shared by Karin in the Facebook group *Allmänheten Diskuterar UFO och UFO-Sverige* in 2022. I like this one. It's mysterious, creepy, and highly personal. And there's something MiB-ish about it, even if she never makes that connection herself.

Kerstin was only eleven years old in 1968, but she clearly remembers that autumn evening. She and her younger brother were home alone; her parents were away playing bingo. Around 11 p.m., she looked out her parents' bedroom window, facing the gravel road outside their house.

She wondered when their parents would come home and was hoping to see their car coming down that road as she stood there. However, what she did see terrified her: in the middle of the road stood a man with a long coat with the collar almost covering his face. He wore a hat pushed down so his eyes were hidden. He had his hands in his pockets, and in front of him, a couple of bright smaller spheres or orbs were flying around. It was a scary and disturbing sight, but it piqued her interest, and she ran down to get her brother so he also could see it.

When they returned to the bedroom, the man was gone. After being mocked for sharing this story on Facebook, she removed her post, and this is all I managed to save.

However, the last thing she wrote before deleting the thread is that she saw the man again but didn't specify where and when.

As usual, the Men in Black are never too far away.

five
night of the ufos

IN THE FOLLOWING CHAPTER, I will go through what might be the biggest and most talked-about UFO flap in Sweden —an event straight out of a sci-fi or horror movie. It involved a family encountering something truly extraordinary, leading to numerous witnesses coming forward, a secret military investigation, and stories that refuse to fade away.

On March 23, 1974, in the community of Vallentuna, north of Stockholm, a strange event occurred—so strange that it's still being talked about almost fifty years later. Hillevi Andersson, who had celebrated her thirty-sixth birthday a few days earlier, was at home with her three children—Cecilia, Elisabeth, and Robert. When some friends canceled their appointment, at 7:30 p.m., she picked up the phone to call her parents, Svea and Hildor, who lived in the area of Orkesta, just a thirteen-minute car drive away, to check on them. For reasons unknown, she couldn't get through, which made her worried. So worried, in fact, that she loaded the kids into the car and drove to her parents' desolate, isolated country home.

While driving up Lindholmen Road to Orkesta, she noticed something in the sky. A strong circular-shaped light seemed to be following Hillevi's car. It first showed up near the Vasa School and was visible until they reached the Orkesta sports field, where it suddenly shrank to the size of an orange and quickly shot up into the sky. They didn't think too much about it. Maybe it was a bright star, a planet, or even a helicopter in the distance. However, the odd light was still on Hillevi's mind as she drove up to her parents' yard at Malmen 5. It was a traditional Swedish two-story red house with white trim, a common sight in the countryside. Her father Hildor met them on the porch and told Hillevi that the telephone was out of order, and the television was suffering from technical interference. The latter annoyed him. It was almost 8 p.m., and with only two TV channels in Sweden, it wasn't uncommon to sit down after dinner to watch the evening news.

Hillevi told him about the light that was following them, and almost instantly they noticed something on the other side of the road, where the old quarry lies. A strong, bright light was hovering above the trees, and beside it, a smaller ball of light was moving in a zigzag pattern. Soon they saw that the lights belonged to some kind of craft: oval-shaped with three beams coming up from the ground into the ship. The whole family froze in terror, and the kids started to scream. Hillevi's daughter threw herself to the ground and refused to get up. Suddenly, once again, the craft shrank to the size of an orange, lifted vertically with incredible speed, and disappeared out of sight. When everyone calmed down, they decided to go to Hillevi's brother, Hilding, in Skrattbacken. It was only five minutes away by car. During the short drive, the alleged UFO was not seen from their point of view. On arrival, Hilding's wife met them outside and immediately asked them about the strange light following their car, something Hillevi hadn't noticed! It was back!

At this moment, both families were scared, and Hillevi decided to leave out of fear and curiosity. After all that had happened, she really wanted to see the strange object again. Hilding took his own car to escort them, but it didn't take long until he saw a hat-shaped object above his car! Not long after, the larger oval-shaped object was observed at a distance of four hundred meters in front of them. It was hovering in the air approximately ten meters above the ground. Hillevi noticed that the smaller orange-colored ball floated nearby. The two objects started following Hillevi and her children. Somehow, in all this terror, curiosity began to grow even stronger, and she parked the car to see what was going on. The light was now above them and filled the vehicle with strong light. Hillevi stopped her daughter from leaving the car. The girl later claimed that something told her to go outside.

After a while, the bright large object went away, but before it vanished, it stopped at a barn, hovered for a while, and then ventured farther out of sight. In total, during the whole evening, Hillevi estimates that she and her family saw the phenomenon for forty minutes.

The day after, Hillevi called the police to report the incident, but they were clearly very skeptical and uninterested. Instead, she called the *Swedish National Defense Research Institute* (*Försvarets forskningsanstalt, FOA*), who politely took down her statement. Their UFO administrator Tage Eriksson, a job he had since 1965, was a hardcore skeptic and suggested it was some kind of balloon—a standard answer he often gave as an explanation for these kinds of observations. In this case, though, his mind was about to be changed. A while later, a representative from the police contacted Hillevi and apologized for how she was treated; she wasn't alone in her strange, otherworldly UFO experience.

The police collected seventy-six reports from thirty-one witnesses in total from March 23 and 24, 1974, all from different parts of the Vallentuna area. Each of them described the same strange, eerie light—and in some cases, as oval- or egg-shaped. A former blacksmith, ninety-year-old Karl Johansson, was convinced the sun had risen early when he saw the craft, as the light was so strong. In the end, there were forty-three days of sightings in the area during the spring that year.

The night before these incidents, school janitor Gösta Häger was going home after a social gathering in Markim. Along his path, close to the ground, he noticed a strange light. It grew increasingly stronger, moving closer to him. Out of curiosity, he walked towards it and was thrown to the ground by a powerful force. A while later, he found himself outside his home in Lindholmen, with a bleeding wound on his head, bruises on his face, and no memory of what had happened to him. He woke up his wife, frantically ringing the doorbell. The day after, he called the National Defense, and they recommended he contact Home Guard chief Hardy Bornholm, who later became more involved in the case as an official investigator and collector of information. On April 1 and May 24 the same year, Gösta met chief physician Ture Arvidsson at the Danderyd hospital and went through two hypnotic regressions. Gösta described how he was taken aboard some kind of craft and was examined by "four transparent men" —in the second session, describing them as Native Americans. They might have worn hoodies, as no noses or ears were visible. The beings gave him a mission, but he was vague about the details, other than it might happen in the year 2000. According to Gösta, they put some kind of instrument against his forehead, which caused a burning pain.

Gösta claimed to have a higher sensibility for precognition and other extrasensory perceptions. This was after an accident in his childhood, where he fell from a tree and lost an eye. Gösta was described as a down-to-earth man who didn't place much importance on his experiences. From the incident in 1974, he received a wound on his forehead and something that was considered burn marks at the time, but they seemed more closely related to bruises. He never claimed his experience was related to aliens. He just didn't know what had happened to him. There were more people who witnessed unexplained phenomena at the same time: a woman on a bike saw a strong light over the same stretch of road, two male witnesses, unaware of each other, saw a metallic object in the field near where Gösta had his encounter. A man and a woman had seen what they first thought was a new water tower, with lights coming out of its top windows. They later understood that there was no such structure there.

Other witnesses experienced bodily pain, vomiting, and migraines. When they sought treatment, the tests showed higher levels of white blood cells—one of the side effects of radioactivity, but also from stress. Hillevi explained it as if she were about to break into two pieces, at the waist. When she returned to the quarry with her husband and Home Guard chief Hardy Bornholm, they found three smaller wedge-shaped marks in the ground, and several trees had lost their tops.

A while later, the National Defense Research Institute arrived in the area. According to witnesses, they were wearing protective clothing and taking samples of burned grass and soil. The commander in chief at the time, Stig Synnergren, ordered the Home Guard to place people in two positions in the area during the weeks that followed. This would enable them to study a possible return of the phenomenon from different angles. It was officially declared a military exercise, "Operation S." According to documents from the Swedish National Defense Research Institute, it was concluded that there was an alleged physical object over Vallentuna that night, but a logical explanation was not given.

What's less well known is that the first sighting had already happened months earlier. It was on January 1 in Torsholma, less than ten kilometers from the later incidents. Early in the morning, a group of four to five people were walking back home from a New Year celebration at a neighbor's house. There was no wind, and it was very calm. Suddenly in front of them, at the edge of a forest, they saw a big cigar-shaped object with a strong luminous light and a row of windows. Depending on whom you ask, the observation lasted from a few seconds to two minutes. It then dissolved and disappeared in front of their eyes. None of them had a logical explanation for what they had seen.

Some of the sightings could have been stars, planets, satellites, and even airplanes coming in and out from Arlanda airport, thirty kilometers away. The close encounter of the oval-shaped craft is, however, not in the realm of those theories and must be considered a mystery. On the downside, the investigation at the time was conducted with a bias towards flying saucers/aliens. This might have affected the memories of those involved: for example, leading questions may have been asked during the hypnosis sessions.

On the other hand, the witnesses have stood by their stories ever since, with little to no details changing over the years. It should be noted that the esoteric connection is strong, both regarding where Gösta Häger was allegedly abducted—an ancient hill, near two runestones—and his overall experiences before, during, and after the incident.

What makes the story even more interesting is that Hillevi had a near-death experience as a child, exactly at the same spot where a UFO hovered near her parents' house. The quarry was used as a place for swimming during the summer. Four-year-old Hillevi fell into the water and lost consciousness. She basically drowned. After being saved by her father, she remembered being surrounded by beautiful lights and a general sense of peace. Is it too much of a coincidence that this, much later, was the place of her close encounter? Hillevi feels this might be connected and that it means something to her.

So what are we dealing with here? Are they extraterrestrials on a visit? Military technology? Some kind of interdimensional leak? A spiritual event?

No matter what the answer might be, the night of the UFOs will continue to be a magnificent mystery.

six

when a flying saucer landed at lake anten

SOMETIMES, when I look back at my writing, I can see how I often focus on so-called inner experiences or dreamlike events, which may or may not be about material objects and beings—things one can touch and sense in a more physical way. Are these nonmaterial visitors or something more tangible, like seeing a car and its driver by the side of the road, and not something from another world? Even famous Swedish UFO flaps, like the one in the Vallentuna area in 1974, have a touch of something from another realm and not necessarily from another planet—even if that case is ambiguous in many ways. So let's take a look at another famous case, which gained a lot of attention at the beginning of the '70s—and still is brought up as a highly interesting example of an alleged landing of a flying saucer or UFO. By the way, may I suggest that we bring back Charles Fort's acronym OSF, objects seen floating, instead? Let's think about it, okay?

At Relsbo Gård, approximately five hundred meters from Enebacken, where the morning after, eighty-one-year-old Rickard Johansson would discover something very strange in his yard, the Karlsson family was just about to go to bed. It was just before midnight on the night between August 29 and 30, 1970, and their life—at least for the moment—was about to change. When Erik Karlsson, the husband, looked out the window, he noticed how a couple of cars on the road below had stopped and turned off their headlights. "Our son came running inside, telling us something bright red and glowing was flying above Enebacken," Erik said. Erik and his wife, Ingeborg, got dressed and went outside to witness the strange sight, and yes, there was something brightly red moving back and forth above the treetops. "At first, I thought it was an airplane, but it couldn't be because of the way it moved. It was round and red," Ingeborg stated to the investigators from GICOFF (Göteborgs Informationscenter för Oidentifierade Flygande Föremål), Björn Högman, Siv Högman, Sven-Olof Fredrikson, and photographer Gunnar Johansson.

The family stood and watched the object for almost two hours, studying its strange movements above the trees. Sometimes it disappeared behind them and then reappeared, and at one moment it was as close as two hundred meters away, down at a field belonging to the farm. Erik and Ingeborg noticed something else; it was like beams were coming out from the red sphere, yellow and white in color. It was about half the size of the full moon from their distance. When they finally went to bed, at two in the morning, the mysterious visitor was still there doing its thing.

During this time, three cars stopped, or at least their passengers reacted to the strange hovering light. Peter Nilsson and his friend were on their way from Alingsås when they saw the red light on the left of the road, above the forest somewhere between 11:15 p.m. and 11:30 p.m. It moved back and forth a couple of times, stopping from time to time. They observed it for approximately ten minutes.

In another car, Marita Olsson and her husband were on their way home from visiting friends in Degerbo when they saw what they thought looked like the light of a car, yellow-red in color, up in the sky. They also thought it was an airplane at first, but the vertical movements made them change their minds. The observation lasted for three to four minutes, beginning at 12:25 a.m.

On their way to Hyttan, Ellen Aronsson and a friend of hers saw a bright, shining sphere on their right side. At first, they mistook it for the moon, but it appeared too red in color. The next morning, Ms. Aronsson visited the elderly Rickard Johansson in her capacity as a domestic helper and was a part of the sensational discovery in his yard.

There were many more reports from that night, most of which described a bright, shining sphere or ball that was red in color and moved back and forth, up and down. One witness said it looked beautiful when it shone its light over the still surface of a lake (possibly Hälsingen, a lake closer to the observation than the more well-known Anten). But it was what came next that truly made headlines in the upcoming weeks of late summer 1970.

The next morning, Ms. Aronsson visited Rickard Johansson's small homestead, Enebacken, positioned around five hundred meters into the forest on a narrow, desolate road, and found that something seemed to have visited his home during the night. On the outskirts of the garden, on the lawn, three prints were clearly visible, placed in a triangular shape with 2.6 meters in between. The word was spreading fast in the area, and already on the day after, twenty or so curious people had visited the spot, some of them taking souvenirs in the form of soil samples. In the weeks after, over one thousand people visited Rickard Johansson's home, which, of course, quickly contaminated the place with footprints and other kinds of damage. However, one thing was clear: the prints that were visible pointed at them being circular in shape, forty centimeters in diameter, and roughly four centimeters deep. According to investigators, the prints were charred and not burned. Surrounded by four trees, the object was calculated to be at most 8.8 meters in diameter, or else the trees would have been damaged by the descent.

Mr. Johansson himself hadn't heard or noticed anything

during the night. His bedroom was on the opposite side of the alleged landing site, on the far end of the house. He went to bed at 9 p.m. that evening and slept well. Contrary to what one might believe, Mr. Johansson actually enjoyed the ruckus surrounding the incident and appreciated people coming around looking at the prints, making him feel less lonely. He wasn't that bothered by possible otherworldly visitors either: "Whoever it is that has landed here, they've been kind and haven't destroyed anything." He added that he had only read about flying saucers in the newspapers, but now he had changed his mind about their existence and would never be in doubt again.

The landing was soon declared a hoax, both by the police and media. *Göteborgsposten* proclaimed, with the headline "The Flying Saucer came from Magra, not Mars," to have the solution. It was, according to them, two teenagers from Magra, around twenty kilometers away, out playing with their hot air balloon, a construction with three jars filled with ethanol. Setting them on fire would result in the balloon rising up into the air. Both boys denied being involved in any mischievous activity, and one of them actually had a solid alibi for that particular night.

Not long after, *Lektyr*, a gentleman's magazine, published their article on the subject, titled "The Hoax of the Year" (possibly as a response to a more positive article in their rival *FIB-Aktuellt*). The article introduced two new chess pieces to the game, a couple of young men from Göteborg, armed with a gas burner, weather balloons, gas tubes, a truck battery, ropes, cables, and everything else they needed to make their hoax work. On GICOFF, this caused some confusion, and their investigators decided to recreate the experiment but felt it didn't live up to what the witnesses saw and the prints left on Rickard Johansson's lawn.

Looking at it with a critical eye, it can be quite easy to dismiss this case—especially since the sensational article published by *Lektyr*. One needs to keep in mind that the magazine was known to create news; it was a populist publication produced only for the sake of selling as many copies as possible, with an audience that craved entertainment before facts. Did they actually construct this story, pay off the boys? No one knows for sure, but the fact is that no one has confessed to being involved in a possible hoax. It's also easy to connect dots that aren't there. An unusually colorful moon, the movement of the eyes against a bright spot in the sky, will create movements that seemingly come from the object itself. A mass sighting of such an event might cause speculation, gossip, and lead to exaggerations—the memory fills in what's not there. The thing is that memory drastically drops in quality after a few hours, and by the end of the day, as much as 50% is gone, and a week later, it's only 10-20% that's there. And where there's a void, there's room to fill in the blanks. One can say that our brain constantly edits our memories, and what you thought you experienced last week is not what you remember today.

That brings us to the prints on Rickard Johansson's lawn. Maybe they have always been there? Maybe they were such a common sight every day that neither Johansson nor his friends noticed them anymore? The word about a mysterious light could have made Ms. Aronsson more attentive to anomalies in her nearest surroundings. Could they have remained after something else, such as fires or construction? It could be like that, of course, but the addition of a mass observation during the night and what seemed like fresh prints, charred and black, the day after just outside his house might seem a bit too much to be a coincidence. The hoax theory is, of course, an important one, but one has to count in the quality of the witnesses and sources, the technical reconstruction by the investigations, even if they might have had a bias towards aliens and flying saucers. I'm not ruling out anything here; everything is possible.

This was the era of mysterious prints in Sweden, and let's take a look at two oddities, a lot less famous than the one above, and the story with which I will end this text. The first one happened —or at least was discovered—on February 2, 1971, by farmer Börje Bergqvist, who was working on his farm, Lillpite, when he noticed an odd pattern in the snow behind the barn. "I'd just moved the hay from the barn and onto the wagon when I saw the rings in the snow outside. I thought it was weird and have never seen anything like it before. I didn't think much more about it, but when I was getting hay again on Wednesday, the rings were still there." It was three circles, the biggest measuring approximately sixty centimeters across. About two weeks later, something oddly similar was found 110 Swedish miles away, in Skoghem, Remmenedal. This time it was farm owner Josef Johansson who found three similar marks, all consisting of three circles inside each other, on the snow-covered barn roof. "I don't believe it was elves or gnomes. They moved north a long time ago. Whatever has left the marks on my barn roof must have come through the air. Moreover, they must have done so since the storm and snowfall subsided on Thursday morning. The marks were not there on Wednesday evening and would have been obliterated by the storm, by the way." The police sent out Inspector Holm, who did a thorough investigation and concluded that the marks couldn't have been made by anyone climbing up on the roof, as there was no sign of intruders around and on the barn. Like the mysterious circle mark in Lillpite, these also had about the same width across, 56 centimeters. In *Alingsås Tidning*, March 12, 1971, seventy-five-year-old Johansson speculated that someone might have bounced against the roof three times and then disappeared.

A case of snow circles instead of crop circles? Investigators from GICOFF had a theory that the first circle was a natural phenomenon, made by the movement of the grass underneath the snow, something they'd seen during the summer. But it's unlikely the same phenomenon would happen in the winter. Let's get back to a few cases without the dreaded snow, and start with one not far from Skirsjön, a small lake in the province of Östergötland. Lennart Engström was out hunting when he encountered an unexplainable mark in the ground. It was located at a very remote location, far from traffic and people, in an abandoned field. The mark itself had a diameter of approximately eighty to ninety centimeters, and the grass was charred, but not burned to the ground. Around the burn mark, Engström found red and white substances. The red was sticky and fat, the white sticky and viscous. In a diamond shape around the burned circle, four imprints were found, around one decimeter in depth. In each of these, a tiny hole was visible into the ground. Vegetation had been uprooted, and it seemed like some kind of vacuum had done this. On a curious note, the area was known since 1967 as a hotspot for all sorts of weirdness, including observations of flying saucers, unexplained engine failures, but also several observations of little people: gnomes, etc. Two boys had witnessed a small figure running into the forest in connection to a mire they visited to pick cloudberries. The little man, as he disappeared from sight, had let out a yodeling.

On August 4, 1976, two boys—Patrik Wegelius and Pierre Stenberg, both fourteen years old—were awake in their beds late into the night, chatting and trying to stay awake as long as possible, as often happens with energetic kids. They were alone in the house belonging to Pierre's grandparents, and when a strong light burst through the windows of the second floor, they first thought the grandparents were coming home. When they didn't hear anyone entering the house, they got up and looked out. What they saw, about 150 meters away from the house, out in a field, was an intense bright light—so strong that it paralyzed them with fear! After a minute or so, they were brave enough to run down to the lower floor to get a better look at what was going on outside. The light started to move sideways, and for a moment it seemed to be moving towards the house. Pierre got scared and called the police, but when the light moved in another direction and then upwards and disappeared, he became calmer.

The next morning, the boys ventured out into the field and found five marks in the ground: four in a square pattern with one burned mark in the middle, and a sixth mark that reminded them more of a hole someone had dug up, not far away. These examples of mysterious marks might seem far-fetched in their connection to the one by Lake Anten, but one case that came up—and caused quite a lot of attention at the time when it happened—was factory director Åke Johansson's strange find outside his summer cabin and former family home in Vänga, seven kilometers outside Fristad, Borås Municipality, on June 6, 1968. What's odd, and for a short while caused some attention among certain investigators, was the name of the owner in Vänga also was Johansson, and the name of his house, Enebacken, was exactly like the one in the Lake Anten case. A third incident involving the same names never happened—as some suggested it would.

One day, Åke Johansson found a big, oily spot on his lawn. He first thought that a motorist had car trouble and dumped oil outside the house. He kind of accepted that thought, even though it was unlikely, considering the location of the spot. Åke, his daughter, and her fiancé arrived in the afternoon and decided to mow the lawn when they found an odd mark underneath the grass.

The next day, the liquid had disappeared, the grass had started to wither on the spot, and a strong, intense, and disgusting smell was spreading. Johansson started to get red spots on his face and hands, and the same thing happened to those who visited him. However, what was really peculiar was that a geometrical shape was beginning to take form on the lawn where the oily substance had been. It consisted of a triangular shape, with another triangle attached at the top—like a double arrow symbol. The first triangle had three circular marks in its corners, and the whole shape had a diameter of 3.1 x 1.6 meters.

Samples of soil and liquid were sent to the agricultural cooperative's research institute, and according to their report, it was neither pesticide, propellant, nor motor lubricant. Chemist Kaj Klarin at the Royal Institute of Technology (KTH) could only find sodium and calcium, common chemicals in soil and nature. Curiously enough, he also ended up getting small wounds and rashes on his fingers and hands after handling the samples.

According to the Johansson family's official WikiTree page,

Åke Johansson was some kind of prepper, and one might wonder if the mark was generated from his work on the site. "The Cold War and Sweden's proximity to the Soviet Union made Åke nervous about the chance of nuclear disaster. He made additions to the property to get it 'off-the-grid,' including the installation of one of the first wind-turbine-powered generators in the area. He kept several enormous tanks of diesel as backup for the imminent disaster. One tank filled a whole shed, and the other was kept in the barn. The barn was Åke's workshop where he'd store and repair old things, tinkering with appliances and other fixtures. One day, the diesel tank or perhaps the fumes in the barn caught fire, and the building was destroyed."

However, for investigator, author, and APRO's Swedish representative K. Gösta Rehn, it was clear: it was a flying saucer that landed on Åke Johansson's lawn, something that he felt was even more convincing after learning that an elderly couple in Ebbared, sixteen kilometers from the landing site, had seen a hovering, floating bright object moving towards the Vänga direction. "One conceivable explanation is that the liquid release is a product of the nuclear operating method, in which liquid metallic elements were precipitated upon landing" was the conclusion he gave the mystery in his second book, *UFO! Nya Fakta om de Flygande Tefaten*, from 1969.

One has to keep in mind that this was during a time when basically all mysterious events in Sweden were alleged flying saucers, and many of these investigations and texts have a strong alien and UFO bias, which in all fairness was the thing in this country during the sixties and seventies. That was the culture, even if it was slowly changing over the next ten years or so. What I love and adore about these stories is the love for the weird, that aliens might have landed on homesteads around Sweden and left strange, unexplained marks on the lawns of surprised homeowners.

Will we ever find out what's behind these incidents? Probably not, and we're left with stories and legends written down by dreamers and believers. I'm not saying that these marks have a natural, rational explanation—oh, no, don't misunderstand me. They might have, but maybe something really did land or crawl up from the depths of the Swedish soil to leave a final imprint before heading back into the unknown realms of our reality.

seven
the boys

THE MOST POWERFUL stargazing experience I've ever had was in South Africa, out on the savannah. As the segment producer for the dating show *Bachelor*, we traveled all around the country, letting the participants eat delicious food, talk, and of course, smooch (when they didn't hate each other), all at the most spectacular locations Kwazulu-Natal could offer. One of the occasions was a dinner for four—a double date with the two bachelors—at the Mavela Game Lodge in the middle of the Manyoni reserve.

I've never seen such an awesome night sky before. The Milky Way was as clear as it's ever been. The only thing that kept me from standing there longer than I did was the sounds of growling lions nearby. Believe me when I say I instantly turned around and walked calmly into the game lodge again without hesitation. I had no wish to wrestle with lions, even under such a stunning night sky.

Around my neck of the woods in Sweden, there's too much light pollution to fully enjoy the wonders of the sky. So each time I'm far away from the big cities and airports, I always take the time to go out and admire the sky after the sun has set. It gives me a sense of awe, a feeling of being a part of something profound and beautiful.

Arriving in the upper north of Sweden is like setting foot on another planet. Mile after mile of forest and rough, rugged plains. On the roads, it can take a long time before you meet another car or truck, and there's even less chance to meet police or any other government-issued vehicle.

During the summer, you'll experience the midnight sun. Going outside at 1 a.m. in the morning and seeing the sun gently glowing above the mountains is a sight to behold. However, during wintertime, the constant darkness is truly extraordinary, when the sky is lit up by billions of stars and embraced by the Milky Way. Watching it makes me contemplate the mysteries of life and the universe, and maybe hope to one day see a moving light up there, something otherworldly and intelligent.

It was under such a sky, on December 18, 1977, that Bruno Nygård had an experience that changed his view of reality. He was on his way home from the nearby village of Kaunisvaara, just a few hundred meters away from his house, when he noticed a dim light above the lonely lamp posts that lined the road. The time was 7 p.m., and he would soon be inside in the warmth again. Well, that is, if it weren't for that strange light above the road, of course.

It was the first thing he noticed, and then on the road itself. Bruno first thought it was two boys on a kicksled, appearing and disappearing in between the light from the lampposts, like a slow-moving strip of film playing out before him. It seemed to be the same very common vehicle he was traveling with himself—but with a large box on the seat. They were on the wrong side of the road, which didn't bother Bruno. 'It's just boys and their inventions,' he thought. The kicksled boys disappeared out of sight shortly, and Bruno continued a few more meters until he could see the carriage again. Now he noticed it wasn't really a kicksled. Instead, it reminded him of a large snuff box: circular, quite flat, and around two meters in width and one meter in height. It was moving forward together with the two dark figures on the sides. They were picking something from the ground, but he couldn't see what. When they saw him, they reacted fast.

By using their hands to support themselves, they jumped perfectly synchronized into the "snuff box" and sat down beside each other. Moments earlier, Bruno had thought they were two boys from the village, but what happened next defied all logic. The "snuff box" suddenly flew straight up, way above the treetops. It rose to around two hundred meters and then made a quick turn to the left, never to be seen again. During the whole flight, it spun, which was visible because of a reflective plate on the front. The center part, with the silhouettes of the two "boys" visible, stayed in place.

"They looked just like people with heads, hands, and feet. But they weren't, that I understood when they jumped inside," he told researcher, author, and journalist Clas Svahn in 1985 for *UFO-Aktuellt*. The whole observation lasted four to five minutes, and he found no traces in the snow afterward.

I think we can all agree that Bruno's observation is a very strange one, and most of it really doesn't fit into the majority of UFO experiences. However, there are similarities to other cases—which I will get back to very soon.

What's interesting is that this area has the highest amount of magnetite, iron ore, in Sweden. UFOs and other strange phenomena are said to be connected to areas with strong magnetism—for what reason, I don't know. Some say it's part of their navigation system, making it easier for them to fly around scaring unsuspecting witnesses. Maybe it makes some of us, during specific circumstances, able to tune into another spectrum of reality?

According to Project Doorway's paper "Positive Magnetic Anomalies and Electron Diffusion Regions in Association with UAP" (Barry Fitzgerald & Steve Mera, 2019), they've come to the conclusion that "through researching well-documented UFO incidents and their locations, it would seem that an extremely high number of reported incidents take place in locations of Positive Magnetic of 100 to 250 nT (nano-teslas)." I decided to check myself and downloaded and installed the EMAG2 filter on Google Earth. With that, it's possible to see the intensity of the magnetic field all over the world, including all the locations mentioned in this book. While a couple of the cases, especially up north (that includes Kaunisvaara, with a positive magnetic of +200 nT), were placed at high-intensity magnetic fields, almost half were on the opposite side of the scale—or even on more neutral grounds. According to Project Doorway, the darker (= negative magnetic field), the higher the risk for criminality and suicide. Considering I'm living in what would be the darkest abyss of magnetism, I guess I'm totally screwed!

In all seriousness, it's all about what you want to see. I guess Project Doorway focused on a specific part of the world, maybe only the United States, and therefore drew the wrong conclusion. Connect the dots in the pattern, and you'll find something to latch on to. It's basically a form of four-dimensional pareidolia.

However, the fact is that the whole upper north of Sweden is filled to the brim with magnetite, and that might, if you're into that, explain some of the weird things. During the ghost rocket period in 1946, a lot of these mysterious rockets were seen up north, over Norrbotten. What makes it more interesting when connecting it to the high level of iron ore is that during July 19, 1946, no less than three of them were seen crashing into lakes in the area: Kattisträsket and Kölmjärv, Överkalix, and Vasarajärvi, Gällivare. There have been later observations of interest. The most fascinating one is from July 1980 when Liz Hellström and Bo Berg were out hiking in the Muddus National Park. They stopped by the Nammajaure lake and witnessed a very spectacular incident. Here's a quote from Bo's diary:

"Then something very strange happened! Suddenly, about one hundred meters above our heads, some kind of missile-like craft swept over our heads at high speed. It flew out over the lake and then made a smooth turn to the left and landed on the water with a big splash and then sank. I think it was about 3 feet long. During the time I saw it, I believed it was an airplane, a cruise robot, or a UFO. It sounded like an airplane, but much weaker. The weirdest thing was that it landed in the lake we were sitting by. Both Liz and I saw it and thought it was weird."

UFO-Sverige has arranged several expeditions to investigate and try to locate the unknown object, but so far, no luck, and the crash is still a mystery.

"The Earth's magnetic field is probably the culprit in many cases of seemingly inexplicable phenomena. Our planet is pockmarked with magnetic anomalies and aberrations," John A. Keel wrote in *The Eighth Tower: On Ultraterrestrials and the Superspectrum*, a collection of insights regarding his theory of electromagnetism and high strangeness. Most of those who have read it would agree it's a seminal work of his—the question is if he's right in his assessment that magnetism has anything to do with the phenomena? Maybe he just got stuck in an idea and never got away from it? It's said that Keel got more and more paranoid over the years, believing beings from the superspectrum were basically stalking him, and that made him stray further and further away from rational thinking. This was of great concern to his friends, who noticed more anxiety in him in his research of high strangeness.

Our brain creates an illusion that we live in a certain consensus reality, and we often think that reality is objective. How can that be so? We're billions of humans, all unique individuals who all see things differently. Of course, there's a lot of shared reality, information, and experiences we feel attracted to and are necessary to even be able to move around in this world. In the end, each one of us sees what's around us—and inside us—through an infinite amount of variants. Like the UFO phenomena has changed shape over the years, so even the culture around it—from the cheesy flying saucers of the '50s and '60s to the visually colder, slicker triangular black shapes and the downright boring Tic Tacs of modern times.

When we see something we haven't seen before, our brain desperately tries to make sense of it. Bruno first saw a detail that was familiar to him at the time of the incident: two boys on a kicksled playing around. Because he had never seen such a thing, it took him some time to comprehend what was in front of him. Even in the end, it might not have resembled what it really was, but transformed into a snuff-box-like craft, a very familiar shape to us in Sweden. Seeing the unknown, stuff we've never seen before, makes us face our own conditioning. When our eyes can't comprehend what we see, we turn to familiar shapes, objects, and archetypes. We think we know, but knowing is a trap we're stuck in until the day we are open enough to look beyond the veil of consensus reality.

Before we go further into our investigation of the unknown (or at least the strange worlds of the Swedish countryside), let's head back in time to Hammerdal, 1961. Valborg and Tilda, two mature ladies on their way home from choir practice one evening, saw something they'd never forget. Afraid of sounding silly, they waited until 1980 to share their story. Well, at least Valborg did—as she had by then lost touch with her friend.

Every Thursday evening, the ladies would leave their homes for a few hours to engage in the beautiful art of choir singing. It was always a night of joy and laughter. None of them would have expected the weirdness that would stop them in their tracks on their way home. After giving a fellow choir member a ride home, they had just left the village of Gisselås when a commotion on the left side of the road, out in a field, caught their attention.

"What the hell is that?" was something Valborg probably didn't say, but from a personal point of view, that's what I would have said. I'm sure Valborg had nicer words to share with Tilda inside the car.

So what did they see?

Approximately 150 meters away, three strange figures stood, dressed in black coats or capes—she compared them to oilskins—and with helmets on their heads. Two of them were maneuvering, or just observing, a tangle of thick cables on the ground. It was like the cables were moving like hoses under water pressure. However, sparks came from their ends. Valborg described them like big, intense sparklers.

In front of this odd scene, a third figure was present, sometimes jumping in between the sparkling cables, and from time to time moving to a mysterious pine tree nearby. Why was it mysterious? Well, because it had a red light in the middle of it—a light that slowly moved up to the top, where it changed color to white, and then went down again and back to red. This was repeated four to five times as the ladies looked with amazement at the strange sight.

After driving closer to get a better look at the scene, the ladies left the car and tried to get there on foot—but bailed out quickly and went home. The next day, as expected, there were no traces whatsoever of the figures, the cables, and what the heck they were doing. The oddest thing though was that there was no pine tree there either. Like the rest of it all, it had disappeared into oblivion.

Was it strangers from another world or just the unique perception of Valborg and Tilda trying to comprehend something they had never seen before—maybe a group of soldiers out on an exercise or technicians trying to fix the telephone lines?

Let's go up into the sky again and leave the ladies on the ground because there is actually another observation in Sweden that is kind of similar to what Bruno Nygård saw during that night.

We need to go back to May 3, 1973, and the town of Mantorp in Östergötland County. The community, consisting mostly of residential homes, is famous for its motor sport arena—but let's not dwell on boring stuff like cars and motorcycles; UFOs are way more fun.

It was 9:45 p.m., and Sigrid Karlsson was out on one last walk with the family dog before bedtime. While the dog was doing dog things, Mrs. Karlsson looked up at the sky, maybe admiring the stars or thinking about what tomorrow would hold. She noticed a red light flying slowly through the night. She didn't think much of it, called the dog, and went home. It was probably an airplane. But she couldn't let go of what she saw. Inside, like the curious lady she was, she glanced through the window and noticed how the red light was still moving around. "That's weird!" She woke up Robert, her eleven-year-old son, who had better eyesight than her. The object was closer this time, around one kilometer from their home, and had stopped over a neighboring house.

The object was pulsating and started to move towards them, in their house constructed on a hill slightly above the other building. The earlier red and intensive color turned to a white-yellow glow, and they could see that the craft was metallic.

As Mrs. Karlsson's eyes didn't have the same sharpness as her son's, she could only see two vertical rods with two dark silhouettes between them. Robert had a much better view with his young and investigative eyes, and to him, it looked like two saucers with their insides towards each other, connected by two transversal bars—and between those, two human silhouettes. "They were looking down at us," Robert said afterward. The object was now about fifty meters away and at a height of around fifty to sixty meters. It passed above, "a little bit faster than a car," and the witnesses ran to the other side of their house to be able to see more. It was now hovering above a field until it flew away and disappeared out of sight. Both Mrs. Karlsson and Robert, separated from each other by the investigators, drew similar sketches of the craft.

The archetypal UFO with two occupants clearly visible has been seen all over the world, often in similarly styled craft. There's a familiarity in this, from the obvious car with headlights and passengers—to the small spaceships used in *The Jetsons*. Is this a physical object or a projection of our culturally biased minds, or something completely unknown? The cartoonish aspect of it, the almost naive design of the craft, makes me think this is connected to the visual backlog of our minds. We see a thing we can't understand and project what would seem fitting at the moment.

Many years ago, we were out walking. It was nighttime, and the rain created a shimmering mirror on the asphalt. In front of us, we suddenly saw a figure on the street, bending down and then up again. It was eerie, like a ghostly phantom moving back and forth in front of us. For lack of better words, it felt supernatural. The closer we got, the more we saw. It wasn't a ghost or alien being; it was a woman rescuing snails from the street and putting them on the grass on the side. Her movements seemed more agile, more smooth in the faint light. We came back to reality again, giggling at the scene we just saw, but impressed by the initiative. Now, imagine yourself out there on a lonely countryside road somewhere in the Swedish winter, lit up by the faint light of billions of stars and a few lamp posts. Suddenly, something appears out of nowhere, something unknown. Just like for Bruno in 1977 or Mrs. Karlsson in 1973.

What would you see?

eight
strangers with candy

SOME SAY THAT SWEDISH PEOPLE, in general, have difficulties accepting gifts, as it means they must give back. Whether that means another gift or some kind of service in return is something to ponder, but I wonder if there might be another reason for it, a reason that goes far back in our folklore. I'll get back to the concept of giving gifts in a moment. Instead, let me introduce you to one of the more enigmatic cases in this book. The place is Västervik, a small town on the edge of Tjust's archipelago in Kalmar County, Småland, and it's the night between December 3 and 4, 1979. Lilli-Ann Karlsson, a sixteen-year-old woman, was turning and twisting in her bed. The moon was bright and powerful, and she felt restless.

Unable to fall asleep, she took a walk in the crisp winter night at the nearby Breviksalperna, a recreational area consisting of a pretty large forest with a hill at the south end of it. During the summer, it is a popular place for picnics, walks, and parties—and during the winter, for skiing and pulk. Tonight it turned into something way more sinister.

As Lilli-Ann walked along the paths circling the area, she was deep in her thoughts when she suddenly felt a strange presence and looked up. In front of her was some kind of craft, oval-shaped and hovering approximately one meter above the ground. Perplexed, she watched it for a while, maybe wondering if it was all a dream.

She sensed that someone was watching her, and moments later, two figures came out from behind the mysterious and very out-of-place object. They were the same height as normal human beings and very slim. Lilli-Ann didn't notice any defined facial features, and they were dressed in tight, white silk-like clothes.

She couldn't move and had the feeling that they were talking about her. "I felt silly and ridiculous," she later told investigator and correspondent Tor Wiklund from *UFO-Information*, and added that she heard a voice telling her not to be afraid. The visitors were laughing at her. "It was as if they thought I looked strange."

As she stood paralyzed, the two beings levitated towards her. They stopped, glanced at each other, and exchanged a few words. One of them stretched out its hand to Lilli-Ann. In the open palm was a gift. She studied it carefully. It looked like, she thought, a chocolate bar.

Lilli-Ann didn't move; she couldn't. Whether it was because of fear is difficult to say. A few minutes later—after seemingly discussing the situation with each other—the beings turned back to their craft, walked behind it, and disappeared suddenly together with it. One moment it was there, and then it was gone.

Free to move again, she ran crying back to her apartment, a home she shared with a friend and her older brother. When her brother came home later from his shift at the local newspaper, Lilli-Ann was still very upset. He encouraged her to seek treatment at the psychiatric clinic, not because of what she saw, but because of her hysterical behavior. Something very serious had happened, and the girl was genuinely scared out of her mind.

When investigators came to the location two days later, there was nothing there to indicate a UFO landing, no burned vegetation or any other traces. The area was visited daily by a lot of people, but no other witnesses could be located.

What really happened to Lilli-Ann is difficult to say, and I will refrain from analyzing her own personal experience too much, as I haven't been able to find and hear her own current opinion on the incident. When asking Tor Wiklund, who met and interviewed the girl, he told me he felt she was telling the truth, a credible witness. While the case itself isn't out of the ordinary compared to other incidents, there's one interesting detail that sticks with me: the gift of chocolate.

As mentioned earlier, some say Swedish people have a difficult time accepting gifts, and maybe that was wise in this case. Could it be that Lilli-Ann did the right thing by not accepting the chocolate? In Joshua Cutchin's excellent *A Trojan Feast: The Food and Drink Offerings of Aliens, Faeries, and Sasquatch*, he mentions a case in France on August 25, 1971, when Paul de Brescia had a very similar situation as Lilli-Ann. Contrary to Lilli-Ann, he accepted the chocolate-like gift and fell asleep in front of the two humanoids. Days later, he woke up back in his apartment. Cutchin also mentions another French case a few years later, in 1974, where a man experienced a very similar thing to the case in Västervik. That time, the beings just looked at him eating the chocolate and then let him go.

During my research on Swedish cases, I haven't been able to locate anything similar to what Lilli-Ann and the French witnesses experienced. The closest case is the fascinating story of Ante Jonsson.

Ante had a terrifying experience in 1984 (which I will discuss in a later chapter) and became a contactee in the years after, up until his death in 2019. In his book from 1989 (co-written by infamous ufologist/Nazi sympathizer/anti-smoking activist Sune Hjort), *Besök Hos Utomjordiska Civilisationer*, Ante describes his journeys into the universe with his new intergalactic friends. To make these trips, he needed to drink a special liquid they gave him. Ante describes this from his first journey: "He extends an arm towards me, and in his hand he has something resembling a mug with something liquid in it. It looks like heavily diluted milk, a little grayish. His hand looks like mine with the difference that no fingers are visible. He wants me to drink. I hesitate, but he insists, so I do as he pleases. It was not very good, a little bland taste, but still sweet. I ask what it is, but get no answer."

On his second journey, a similar thing occurs, but this time the visitor explains more: "When I sat down, a fifth figure came into the room and gave me a mug with that drink I had received before. I wonder what it is, but say nothing. I still get answers from the pale man. He says I have to drink from this because otherwise, I will not be able to make the journey we are going to make. I ask where we are going and why. He explains that we are going to travel to the same planet as last time, but I'll be back before morning."

More than a year later, in preparation for a longer trip, he was given a bottle with the liquid and was told to drink it to be able to endure the long journey. In Earth time, he would be gone for thirteen hours, but in their time, it would be six days.

In Celtic mythology, there's a recurring tradition of not accepting gifts from otherworldly beings such as forest spirits, fairies, elves, gnomes, goblins, and so on. The offering of food doesn't just symbolically represent a connection between the giver and the receiver but also a physical, tangible connection. Eat the food they serve, and they will forever be in your presence—or in the worst case, follow them for a snack, and you might never come back.

In Swedish mythology, it is mainly believed that you should never accept an invitation to dance with the elves and fairies. However, food and drink may also be offered, as in the story told by twenty-two-year-old farmhand Jacob Jacobsson.

On September 16, 1759, Jacob Jacobsson testified to Rev. Vigelius about how he was on his way home after delivering food to a farmer. After crossing a lake with his boat, he found a large and broad road he had never seen before. Young, curious, and somewhat foolish, he followed it until he came to a grand, red mansion. Soon he found himself sitting on a bench in a large chamber. In front of him, at the end of a table, sat a small chubby man with a red hat. Around them was a frenzy of little people running back and forth. Elves were also present, eating, and a beautiful maiden his own size. She offered him food and drink. Jacob finally sensed something was wrong and refused to accept their delicious gifts. He asked God to take him home. This upset the little people, and they threw him out of their gathering, saying, "Throw him out, he has such a foul mouth!" When he finally arrived home, after first finding himself at the shore of the lake, he learned he had been gone for four whole days!

One person who had better luck was Mrs. Rahm and her husband, Petrus. One evening in 1666, a small man walked into their home in Ragunda and asked for help. They suspected he was either a troll or vätte. The strange man said his wife was about to give birth and needed help. After some persuasion, as he asked her four or five times, Mrs. Rahm reluctantly agreed. Blessed by her husband's prayers, she got dressed and followed him. Outside, it felt like she was "taken by the wind" into the night. Soon they arrived at a small cottage. Deep inside, in a small dark chamber, a small woman was in pain. Mrs. Rahm helped the odd couple with the birth as best she could. Afterwards, the small man offered her food. Already suspicious that the man wasn't human, she refused and left.

Outside, she was once again brought back to Petrus in their home the same way she departed. What would have happened if she had accepted the food? One thing that might indicate the small man had friendly intentions was the gifts found in their home the day after, several silver spoons.

As in the case of Ante Jonsson's contact and, overall, a common thing with alien abductions, time passes differently—a few hours can seem like days! Another example worth mentioning is Hejnumkällingen, a woman (actually a merge of two generations of women during the nineteenth century) on the island of Gotland. She was accused of being a witch and was called to the priest for interrogation. According to her, at the age of ten, she was abducted by "di sma undar jordi," the small ones under the ground. Down there, they tortured her with blows and pinches (which in itself is similar to modern UFO abduction cases)! What's even more interesting is that she met another human in their realm, a woman who warned her not to eat anything she was being offered down there.

In Jacques Vallée's 1969 groundbreaking book, *Passport to Magonia: From Folklore to Flying Saucers*, the famous computer scientist and ufologist examines the connection between folklore and modern UFO experiences. He brings up the famous Eagle River incident on April 21, 1961, where plumber and part-time chicken farmer Joe Simonton discovered a chrome-colored craft outside in the yard of his farm. The humanoids (looking like Italians according to him) came out and asked for water. He brought them a cup (given to him by them) from his well. They then continued to make pancakes and invited him to eat with them, which he did. "If that was their food, then God help them, because I took a bite of one of 'em and it tasted like a piece of cardboard."

Obviously, the aliens didn't have the same talent for cooking as the Italians they looked like. Skeptics, both for and against the UFO phenomenon, lean towards the theory that he might have just had a dream, maybe a lucid one, and somehow mixed the unconscious and conscious reality. But that doesn't really explain the physical fact of pancakes. Did he make them while under the influence of dreaming? It could be, but it seems unlikely.

Simonton later said that he regretted telling anyone about the experience, as, not unexpectedly, people didn't believe him. It's these details that fascinate me—why make up such a ridiculous thing if you want to be taken seriously? Why did Kjell Näslund describe the beings as fuzzy, levitating boxes? What's the reason for Bruno Nygård to even tell about the boys and their flying snuff box? Lilli-Ann told both the press and investigators that she was offered a piece of chocolate by two aliens—an absurd story by any means.

It's not a new theory, but the longer I've been looking into the phenomenon, the more I feel the witness experience is something highly subjective. It's like the event takes place in a nonphysical/part-physical reality that phases into our reality from... somewhere else, all connected to human consciousness. The UFO phenomenon has changed drastically over the years, and so have the experiences of the witnesses. It seems like what they see is deeply connected to their own points of reference. In 1897, hundreds of people saw mysterious airships in the skies, sometimes landing—and even with passengers that seemed "foreign or talked with a strange language.

In Sweden during the 1930s, peaking around ''36 and '37, hundreds of reports came in of unknown airplanes flying over the country, sometimes landing—but always getting away before anyone arrived. Much of these could be explained by misidentification of stars, planets, bolides, and other kinds of space-related phenomena, but still, airplanes. That was what people had in mind during the time.

During 1946, once again in Sweden, there was a huge rash of ghost rocket sightings—a well-known case in ufology. This time it was after the war, and the space age was just beginning to bloom, and people had that in mind—there was no talk about aliens and UFOs yet in the bitter north. The phenomenon was (and still is) in many countries connected to religion, spiritual experiences, and folklore—but it began to change in Sweden during those years. And so did what people saw.

What's familiar to people, their consciousness merges with. The experience itself becomes a projection of their own existence, whether it's by conditioning through culture and religion, or their own personal experiences and reference points. I'm not saying this is so, but it's a hypothesis that works no matter if you're into folklore, ufology, cryptozoology, or whatever makes your heart beat a little bit extra. It's a pity these fractions of subcultures often look at each other with skepticism; a gnome to someone is as impossible as an alien to someone else—and vice versa.

Looking at the case of Lilli-Ann, it was probably a smart thing not to accept the food from the alleged aliens. Maybe that's why her case is still unknown, and Joe Simonton is still being talked about among those interested in the subject? For Joe, it was something he would never do again because of the ridicule. In this way, he became forever connected to his visitors, just like so many in European folklore.

I had another thought while looking into this and other cases involving candy, food, and drink. Is the everlasting parental warning to not accept candy from strangers a caution that came out of folklore—intertwined with experiences like the one Lilli-Ann had? Is it connected to the Boston clown panic that started in May 1981? Men dressed as clowns were driving around offering kids candy, clowns with machetes chasing children through forests, half-naked clowns trying to lure the little ones into vans—stories that would hint that they would be kidnapped and subjected to all kinds of horrendous torture if accepting the gifts. None of those stories was proven to be real. Once again, there were lots of witness reports—but not one single piece of evidence. Cryptozoologist Loren Coleman coined the theory of the "Phantom Clown" during the same time and found out it was a nationwide phenomenon, spreading throughout the United States. In the end, it was explained as something from the mind of the children. By the way, imagine if the phantom clowns were treated the same way as UFOs and aliens? Would we have clown-tactees instead of contactees?

Children are less conditioned by what is real or not, and they tend—or claim—to see things that we adults do not. It is very possible that this type of perception of reality works for those of us who have been able—at least in part—to free ourselves from the conditioning of previous experiences and the flow of objective information.

Hysteria, dimensional rifts between realities, or spectacular projections of the collective consciousness? Elves offering food to a farmhand, aliens offering pancakes to Joe Simonton, aliens offering chocolate to Lilli-Ann, and clowns offering candy to children—it's all so damn similar.

nine
reality shift

WHEN IT COMES TO SWEDEN, you can count on one thing: the relentless human pursuit of sunshine. In a country where it's dark and cold for six months every year (during the wintertime up to twenty 20 hours of darkness up north per day), most people do basically everything to barbecue themselves under the sunbeams. This goes extreme during the summer months, June to August. Everyone is outside.

Those lucky enough to have been born in the '40s or '50s could easily get a cheap summer house located at the most idyllic spots one can imagine. Nowadays, a run-down, moldy cabin in the woods can be so expensive I don't even dare to mention it. However, the sun, this glowing inferno of deliciously boiling fire, is (so far) for free. Its during that time of the year we meet the heroes of this story.

Veikko Tupasela and his fiancée, Lena Manninen, were probably at the beginning of their vacation and decided to spend it the best way possible: on an island in the Stockholm archipelago. Their friend Paavo Mekelä and Veikko's dog, Merisse, joined them on the relatively short trip from Penningby in Norrtälje municipality to the island of Furusund. From there, they would continue by boat to a remote cabin on a small islet not far away, Stor Furen.

The Stockholm archipelago is the biggest in Sweden, with twenty-four thousand islands and islets. Its current shape wasn't visible until the Viking age. The archipelago is always in a state of change, from the first trembling post-glacial movements up until today. The landscape is a sight to behold, with nature and water in all directions. The road from Penningby to Furusund goes over several bridges, connecting the islands with each other.

Our three friends were laughing and enjoying their trip when they arrived at a part of the road built on an embankment. There's water on both sides, with a shorter bridge connecting to the island of Solö. The road is pretty narrow, and when they noticed a Volvo on the other side, they slowed down and pulled into the side of the road for a few seconds to let it pass. For a moment, the view of the approaching car was blocked by the slightly elevated top of the embankment and bridge.

They waited, but the Volvo didn't show up. After a few moments, they started the car and drove slowly up the narrow road and onto the bridge. No Volvo was to be seen. The time was 6:30 p.m., and it was still bright outside, as usual during the summer months.

Afraid there had been an accident, they searched the bridge to see if there was any broken fence, but it was intact. They drove around in the area for a while, still looking for the car, and found nothing that would indicate either an accident or a hidden parking spot. All of them had seen the approaching vehicle very clearly, brown with a blue roof, and the sudden disappearance of it shook them to the core. There was no trace of it! Did reality pull a prank on them?

Their mood got better the closer they got to Furusund, and soon the mysterious car was nothing but a faded memory. Their motorboat was waiting, and it was time for a couple of days at the cabin with fun and chill. The Swedish summer was there to be enjoyed to the fullest.

After arriving at the islet of Stor Furen, they settled in and could finally relax in the sauna after the absurd incident earlier during the day. It wasn't until somewhere between 10:45 and 11:30 p.m. that their existence once again was interrupted—this time by a gunshot, and then a second one! At least, that's what it sounded like.

This was a surprise to Veikko and Pavo, who both sat on the terrace, enjoying the summer evening. Who was shooting at this time and in a place like this? Veikko turned his eyes east and saw something absurd! In a birch tree grove not far away, the Volvo Amazon, brown, and with a blue roof, was visible! This was impossible, as there were no cars nor roads on the islet.

The vehicle moved deeper into the grove and disappeared in a fraction of seconds. Moments later, they both could hear and see movement in the vegetation. Veikko compared it to an enormous invisible hand slowly pushing down the trees, all in the same direction. The thickest of them broke like a matchstick one meter above the ground. After a few minutes, most of the trees slowly bent back to their original shape. During the ruckus, Veikko hastily went inside, found his camera, grabbed his boots, and ran outside.

When the men got closer to the grove, the last of the trees returned to their original state, and all that was left was the broken one, which were so thick that it was difficult to wrap one's arms around them. Veikko's dog, Merisse, who was with them all the time, didn't react until they got closer to the vegetation. It started to growl and assumed a defensive position by lying down straight towards the trees. The evening was once again calm and peaceful, and Veikko and Pavo retreated to their cabin. The next morning, a couple of neighbors joined them, inspected the area, and could see how impossible it was for the tree to break by itself. What a compelling start to the vacation!

Most of the cases brought up in this book are set during wintertime, but not this one. However, once again, we have events that happen outside of crowded areas, in peaceful and calm environments. The minds of the witnesses are more relaxed and, maybe, more open to otherworldly manipulation. Veikko didn't only compare the spectacular finale of their strange summer saga to a huge invisible hand, but he also added that it looked like some kind of low-flying invisible craft taking off.

The stillness, at least from my childhood memories of being out with the family boat in the archipelago, struck me as powerful and almost creepy, like I was completely alone in the universe. Today, with more houses being built, millionaires buying up attractive seaside property, and tourists partying on the beaches and shorelines, it's a different thing. The zones of silence are slowly becoming extinct, though it's still, compared to the larger communities around, quite peaceful.

Disappearing cars aren't new in the annals of UFO history, and one worth mentioning is the case Jenny Randles and Derek James bring up in *Flying Saucer Review*, 1977. The incident happened in 1971 when a man called the police, worried he might be surveilled by two men in a black Jaguar: "The patrol car was parked on the main road just away from where the Jaguar was standing. The police officers got out and walked towards the Jaguar and its occupants. They came up to it and were about to knock on the window when the car and its two passengers simply disappeared, as if they had melted away in front of the eyes of the astonished policemen. The area was examined, but there was no way in which the car could have disappeared naturally, and in any event, the police officers were close enough to be quite positive as to what had transpired."

It's a disappearing car for sure, but the event is very different from what Veikko, Lena, and Paavo experienced. So let's go outside the box for a moment and put ourselves inside a car instead, one that possibly got lost into another realm.

My first real job was as an assistant at TV4 Jämtland, a local TV station. One day, after doing nothing of importance to get myself a job or anything constructive with my life, a new acquaintance named Jan called.

Jan Kerbosch is a colorful, straightforward Dutchman who served as the advertising producer at the station at the time. He's a man of many talents, a former rock star, troubadour, actor, and everything in between. He asked me if I was interested in a job—and so my career in television began. We got along well and have kept in contact during the years since. The last time we talked—me checking if he knew about any haunted places on Öland—the island where he lives—he suddenly told me a strange story about a car ride he and his son once did. A car ride that took them way out of their comfort zone.

After finishing up shooting a music video at Mellby Ör Inn for one of his recordings, Jan and his son, Joel, took the road back to Mörbylånga. While Jan isn't sure of the date, it was either December 20 or 21 (on a curious note, December 21 is the winter solstice, the longest night of the year), at around 9:15 p.m., and darkness had fallen. It wasn't especially cold outside, around +3°C, and the fog was rolling in over the flat island, known for its lack of hills and mountains. A dream for lazy cyclists like me and a place that wears its dusty spaghetti-western aura with pride.

As the fog had thickened, and its color turned from the classic —for the island—blue to an eerie yellow-green tint, Jan drove slower and more carefully than usual. They didn't want to end up hitting an animal or a person on a night like this.

"Have you seen the road sign to Mörbylånga?" he asked Joel and got a negative answer. Something was off because they hadn't seen ANY road signs for quite some time. The signs are usually easily visible because of their reflective properties, even during a foggy night like this. There should be at least ten or fifteen of them on this stretch of road, but nothing was to be seen.

Suddenly, it dawned on them that there were no lights around. The street lamps were either off or invisible, and the passing houses were dark. The only way they could see what was ahead was through the headlights of their car. "It felt like we were in a bubble, separated from reality," Jan recounted later.

Then they noticed something strange. The roads on Öland are flat, so they were both surprised when the road suddenly sloped downwards at an angle of maybe eight to ten degrees. The road continued like this for several kilometers. After a while, they came to an area that looked familiar but still felt wrong.

As they drove north, there should have been a farm on the right side, but now there was nothing there except a greenhouse with white windows. "“I had a strange, disturbing feeling that something horrifying was happening in there, and I don’t want to know what it is!” Jan’s gut feeling grew stronger as he considered turning back the way they came. “Something was coming from behind us. Not a ghost, maybe nonhuman, a physical being—and it was after us.” With this in mind, they continued forward until they noticed forests of fir trees on both sides of the road, in an area where there shouldn’t have been any. Jan even stepped out of the car and could smell the trees.

As they kept driving, lights appeared in the distance, and they slowly recognized the town of Mörbylånga in front of them. The fog returned to its normal color. They were once again safe.

When Jan came home to his partner at the time, Lena, he couldn’t stop talking about their experience—but there was zero interest in discussing it. Not even Joel feels comfortable talking about it up until today.

“It’s like it never happened,” Jan said.

One thing I find interesting is the dates, which are connected to the winter solstice. According to some cultures around the world, the winter solstice is the time when demons, ghosts, trolls, sinister spirits, and all kinds of critters and creatures are able to penetrate the realms between their reality and ours. Was it an entity like that Jan sensed coming for them?

British researcher and investigator Jenny Randles dedicated an entire book, *Time Storms: The Amazing Evidence of Time Warps, Space Rifts & Time Travel*, to this kind of phenomenon, and judging by the amount of incidents brought up through her research, it’s not uncommon. In her 1983 book, *UFO Reality*, she first tries to define these experiences: “I call it ‘the Oz Factor,’ after the fairytale land of Oz. I do not know whether this analogy is helpful or misleading, but it is as if a spell is cast by the famous magician from that land, taking the witness into a new reality. In one form or another, the Oz Factor is very common. What we must do is follow the yellow brick road in search of the wizard."

Many of the details Jan and his son experienced—the hard-to-define shift in consciousness, the silence, the feeling of being in a bubble outside our objective reality, and so on—are also present in the majority of the cases where witnesses enter this form of reality shift. Those who criticize the concept of the Oz Factor often bring up that the state of shock involved in accidents often gives a feeling of separation and being cut off from the outside reality. In most—if not all—of the cases Randles brings up, the shift just happens without any accident or trauma involved from the start.

The closest thing I've been to a similar experience was very mundane, but after all these years, I still remember it as if it were yesterday. Grzegorz and I were feeling hungry one evening and decided to leave the apartment to take a short walk to a nearby Thai restaurant. It was humid outside, and a faint mist greeted us, which made for a cozy and magical walk towards our destination. When we arrived at the restaurant, we noticed how empty it was—and it was quite a spacious place, consisting of one big L-shaped room. What caught my attention was the only other guests, sitting right inside the entrance by a round table: an almost cartoonish chubby family consisting of a man, a woman, and two children—a son and daughter. They ate in silence with their heads down. We soon realized that the whole atmosphere in the food establishment was thick with dread. It felt dense in there, a strange feeling of being very off. The staff seemed detached from what they were doing, and the usual joy was gone. Finding our visit a bit uncomfortable, we enjoyed the food as quickly as we could and left the restaurant. Just as we were leaving, I heard a voice calling out to me from the doorway. I turned around. It was the man from the round table. He repeated his words to me: "Did you think this was a speed eating competition?" Confused by his words, I mumbled something back about us being very hungry and quickly closed the door behind us.

On the surface, mundane is the perfect word to describe this experience, but everything was so unreal, dreamlike, and absurd. Like we were participants in a movie or a setup. Was the place being robbed without our knowledge and everyone just pretending to do what they were doing? Maybe. The restaurant, a pretty good establishment, closed down soon after this incident—like so many other hopeful, ambitious entrepreneurs renting these specific facilities for their culinary projects.

But what really happened to Jan and Joel that December night in 2013? Jan has thought a lot about it, "If I were to speculate, the only thing I would think about is that I ended up in a parallel universe. Why, I don't know, but it's the only thing that sounds fun, if you understand what I mean? I ended up on a parallel Earth where something had happened."

Jan is a driver by profession, and he knows the roads on Öland like the back of his hand. He doesn't use drugs and only a moderate amount of alcohol, and of course, never when he's driving. He knows what he and his son experienced, and he will never forget it.

Did Veikko, Pavo, and Lena witness an event similar to Jan's from an outsider's point of view? They saw a few short, incoherent appearances of a car, but from the driver's side, a hellish road trip that never seemed to end? A rift in time and space from two different positions, like dimensions phasing in and out of each other at the outer limits of a twilight zone.

A few months after I did the interview with Jan, I got a surprising email. It was from my uncle Göran, a well-known ornithologist living on the same island. One night, on July 13, 2022, he and his partner, Annelotta, had been outside to listen to the eerie sound of the European nightjar. Unlike Jan, they had found the correct stretch of road, from Alby to Södra Bårby (which happens to be the same road Jan had planned to use) and found themselves driving kilometer after kilometer on an apparently endless road. A familiar environment had become alien, a stretch of road they'd driven many times before turned into a dreamlike experience where time and space seemed to have set them astray.

In the end, Göran and Annelotta discovered they had ended up four kilometers fartherfurther to the west than estimated, and that five minutes had been lost, which was very strange because of their familiarity with the area. It wasn't possible for this to happen, but it did. Like Jan, they finally managed to orientate themselves and found their way back to the waiting nightjars.

Just another night on Öland, at the fringe of reality.

ten
aliens attack!

IN UFOLOGY, the contactee culture can almost be religious in its view on visitors from outer space—or any other esoteric plane of existence preferred. It's not uncommon to find theosophists, occultists, and other kinds of spiritualists among the channelers of Venusian angels, Nordic aliens, and other so-called higher beings.

One can say it already began with the Swedish scientist, philosopher, and mystic Emanuel Swedenborg. In 1758, he published *De Telluribus in Mundo Nostro Solari, quæ vocantur planetæ: et de telluribus in coelo astrifero: deque illarum incolis; tum de spiritibus & angelis ibi; ex auditis & visis*, also known as the less complicated *Earths in the Universe*. In the book, he reports on his spiritual journey through the universe, an adventure told with as complicated and long-winded sentences as possible.

At least we learn that the inhabitants on Jupiter love good conversations and are not shy of being naked. Sounds like a perfect way of living, if you ask me. Much later, new Swedish channelers descended into our realm. Sture and Turid Johansson are two of them. More on them later. Let's instead focus on a different kind of contact person, Ante Jonsson, whose introduction to intergalactic communication was quite spectacular.

Most contactees started their relationship with the wonderful world of aliens and flying saucers in very ethereal and peaceful ways: a flying saucer lands somewhere near a lake, a blond Nordic-looking Venusian with annoyingly generic facial features floats out from his or her spaceship with a message of peace, love, and cryptic promises of big things coming ahead. However, Ante's life as a contactee started with a horrifying incident, as far from the typical first-time contactee experience as possible.

It was on February 3, 1984, and Ante Jonsson was on his way home by car along the icy, snowy roads from Ingelstad to his home in Tingsryd. It was close to 1 a.m. in the morning, and he wanted to get some sleep after spending the evening with friends. The poor visibility made him slow down, and when he arrived next to a field, a few kilometers from the community of Väckelsång, he knew it was a risky place. He didn't want to encounter the white shark of the Swedish roads: the not-so-carnivorous humongous moose.

Nobody wants half a ton of a hairy, horned beast crashing through their windshield! Contrary to popular belief, it's not just the weight (up to seven hundred kilos) of such an animal that poses a danger. The chance of stomach acids pouring out from a ripped-up belly, all over the unlucky driver, is a significant risk. Ouch.

He didn't see any moose that night, neither carnivorous nor vegetarian. Instead, it was a dark, short figure walking by the side of the road. He didn't give it much thought at the time. Something much more sinister would soon steal his attention.

Just before reaching a field, he noticed something on the far end of the pasture, and he cranked down the car window to get a better look. At a distance of one hundred 100 meters, he saw a huge black object in the darkness. It was still very visible at night, illuminated by the snow. He estimated it to be around eighty meters long and ten meters in height. It looked like a submarine with sloping ends and an increase in the middle. In contrast to a typical submarine, it was hovering not far above the ground.

Ante, an avid amateur photographer, discovered that he had forgotten his camera at home! He quickly drove home to get his camera, hoping the object would still be there when he returned. His wife woke up as he dashed into their bedroom to get his equipment. He told her what he had seen and left.

An interesting detail is that his wife was sure he told her he saw the object together with another man. Did he refer to the dark figure walking on the road, maybe another witness? Ante later denied he had mentioned another man to his wife.

Back at the field, he discovered the object had disappeared. The visibility was now better, and he decided to drive around to see if it was still around somewhere. After searching for a while, he gave up and was about to turn the car around when he had to step on the brakes out of sheer surprise. In front of him, at the crossing between the road he was on and the main one, another object was hovering. It was similar to the first one, just smaller: fifteen to twenty meters in length and five to ten meters in height.

His car, a Saab 99, spun around and stopped just a few meters from the object. It had three bulges underneath at the bottom, and the color was matte black. It was a frightening sight, especially when it was so close. For obvious reasons, Ante wanted to get out of there. While turning around the car, he lost control once again and skidded into a snowbank along the road. This time he got stuck.

Looking up at the terrifying sight again, he felt relief. It was gone. He still wanted to get the hell away from there, which was easier said than done. Stuck in the snow, and the car wouldn't move! When opening the door to step out, to push the car to freedom, he felt something grabbing his left arm with force. It was a short being, dressed in a cloak and hood, no less than sixty to ninety centimeters in height. It almost looked cubic in shape, both body and head. Was this the creature he had seen walking beside the road earlier?

The creature, or whatever it was, violently pulled him out of his vehicle! Ante screamed for his life and struggled to get loose from the hard grip. Soon he managed to free himself and ran towards a couple of nearby houses. His escape route was stopped by a couple of other identical creatures coming up from the roadside. They attacked him, dragging him with them while pulling his clothes. He soon saw why. Farther away, a similar matte black object—or maybe the same as the one he almost crashed into minutes before—stood waiting. He had the terrible feeling that they wanted to bring him aboard.

Ante panicked and fought for his life! Unexpected help came from a big truck slowly driving by without noticing the drama. The strong lights scared the creatures, and they released their grips and disappeared into the night. Exhausted, he stumbled back towards his car, fell down, and crawled the rest of the way—and then he didn't remember anything until he woke up at Växjö hospital.

In all honesty, the story has changed a bit over the years, both from Ante himself and in different newspaper articles written about the incident. However, there are very interesting details that make it—in some parts—believable. The statement from his wife, how he came home in the middle of the night grabbing his camera, is one, but the most interesting is how at 1:50 a.m. the same morning, a call came to the Växjö police department. A man introducing himself as Bengt Johansson reported that he had seen a car by the road, stuck in the snow with its headlights on, and above it, a black object was hovering. Bengt, that's what he called himself, at least found the nearest telephone booth and promised to stay until the police arrived, which he didn't, and he has never been identified. There were no more traces outside the car than the ones of Ante himself. He was found sitting in a deep state of shock, convulsively grabbing onto the wheel. According to himself, the authorities first suspected he was a spy out photographing military installations during the night. Little did he know that the area—and specifically the actual road itself—was a military zone! The road had been widened to be able to let airplanes take off and land during wartime.

Ante called bullshit on that accusation. Instead, he contacted the media not long after about how badly he was treated by the police, hospital staff, and the military. In his opinion, they should focus on investigating aliens and not him.

Another thing worth mentioning is the silence. A compact silence, unusually calm according to Ante. The only thing he heard was a dog barking in the distance. Is it the Oz factor playing a tricky game again, that sudden vacuum in reality that so often embraces the witnesses? This might be the case of the area itself, a rumored hotspot for the paranormal. In an interview a few days after the news broke, Gustaf Johansson, who at the time had lived on the edge of the field since 1924, confirmed it was so with two anecdotes.

On the property are two prehistoric grave mounds, which piqued the interest of a local man. He had started to remove stones from a mound when he suddenly saw how his farm was on fire, engulfed in flames! The grave robber dropped everything and ran towards his home... only to see how there was no fire at all! Another story is how Gustaf's brother-in-law was out walking one night and saw the glow of a cigarette coming towards him. The glow got closer and closer, and he noticed it was floating in the air. Just when it was beside him, it suddenly disappeared.

Other witnesses claimed to have encountered UFOs in the area afterwards, but nothing competes with what Ante experienced on that cold February night.

It's interesting how many of these incidents in this book are set during wintertime, the majority of them between December and March. Incidents that are extra weird, visually impressive, and have a higher strangeness factor than usual. Is it the magical appearance of the Swedish wintertime that plays tricks on people's minds—the darkness, the cold, the overall mood that strikes us who live here? Maybe it's the environment itself that attracts these odd and otherworldly experiences? Truth be told, I have no idea. I can only speculate. What's your take on it?

The experience Ante Jonsson had didn't end there; instead, it set off a series of events that followed Ante for the rest of his life. Over and over again, he was contacted by alleged entities from beyond our world, most of them humanlike, very polite, and friendly. Unlike many other contactee cases, they didn't seem to want him to relay their messages to the public. Except for one time, but like everything else in his story, he kept it very much to himself.

Most of the communication he received dealt with himself and his personal development as a human being. They brought him gifts consisting of technical equipment and stones. He was told to keep the gifts to himself because all had value in his relationship to them.

Once again, folklore comes to mind. Jacques Vallée mentions in *Passport to Magonia: From Folklore to Flying Saucers* that gifts coming from grateful elves often had magical properties. A gift of coal in a Chinese tale was transformed into pure gold (for us humans, an oddly appreciated metal), and a German woman found her apron full of the same beloved metal after an elf encounter.

The contactee culture took off during the 1940s, following the flying saucer wave that came with Kenneth Arnold's sighting, the alleged crash in Roswell (both in 1947), and of course, Thelemite and bon vivant Jack Parsons' famous rocket experiments. Some say Parsons, by his occult practices (starting with Aleister Crowley's contact with the suspiciously Gray-esque entity Lam in 1917), opened up portals, giving non-worldly entities wider access to our reality.

Science fiction movies started to get produced, all involving space travel, imaginatively visualized distant planets, and weird and campy-looking alien monsters. Directors and producers like Jack Arnold, Ray Harryhausen, George Pal, and many others shared their vision of the unknown and were forever cemented in the memory of mankind. The Russians were already at it in 1924 with Yakov Protazanov's *Aelita*, and in Vasily Zhuravlev's *Cosmic Voyage* from 1935. Oh, and not to forget Georges Méliès' seminal

1902 short film *Le Voyage dans la Lune*, known to the international audience as *A Trip to the Moon*.

Contactees such as George Adamski, George Van Tassel, Howard Menger, and Billy Meier (whose Swedish representatives I met in 2021—a friendly and almost shy group of individuals who undoubtedly practiced the concept of non-mission that Meier proclaimed is the correct thing to do) all preached peace and love, connecting with beautiful Venusian women, and essentially started the modern New Age culture. Eventually, this movement made its way to Sweden. Sten Lindgren founded the Intergalaktiska Federationen (IGF) in 1965, and with him came several personalities who claimed to be in contact with space brothers and star people. The most well-known of them may be the known hoaxer and pathological liar Daniel Glantz, who combined his deep Christian faith with wild stories of UFO landings, close encounters of the third and fourth kinds, and the claim that Jesus was the boss of the space brothers. It was a closed circuit of strange personalities with certain tendencies toward cult behavior. Håkan Blomqvist, who was once invited into the secretive world of the IGF as a teenager, shared his experience: "On November 21, 1970, my schoolmate Kjell Jonsson and I were initiated into the Venusians'' secret operations in Sweden and the spiritual philosophy of the space people. Sten and Bjarne turned off the lights in the apartment, and while we listened to 'cosmic music' from an organ, the sound was combined with a color spectacle on the wall. Everything was sacred, spiritual, and mysterious. It was intended that we be brought together, Sten explained. Two neurotic teenagers were saved at that moment. Life took on a higher meaning. I thought this was Shangri-La."

Jacques Vallée defines the contactee like this: "I call the indirect contactees, people who have convinced themselves of the existence of an intelligent cause that can produce unexplained phenomena, have not observed such phenomena themselves, but feel that they have some kind of personal link to this cause nonetheless, one that again gives them a special destiny among mankind. In this category are all the people who receive messages from outer space by automatic writing or other means, but have not seen a UFO, and those who simply consider themselves as having been given a 'cosmic mission' by the superior intelligence in question" (Messengers of Deception: UFO Contacts and Cults, 1979).

Jacques Vallée has a quite dark and pessimistic view on this subculture and never really ruled out the esoteric connection, as does John A. Keel. Both seem to agree that one negative aspect of the phenomenon is that it deliberately takes control over easily manipulated people to spread confusion, disinformation, and can be dangerous with its trickster personality. This proved Vallée to be correct while investigating, in the above-mentioned book, Bonnie Nettles and Marshall Applewhite and their H.I.M. (acronym for Human Individual Metamorphosis) cult in the '70s. It later transformed into Applewhite's notorious Heaven's Gate. No, not Michael Cimino's famous 1980 box office flop, but the cult. With brand -new Nike shoes on their feet, a five-dollar bill, and three quarters in their pockets, they were supposed to transcend to a spaceship, accompanying the Hale-Bopp comet. It didn't work out, it seems. The saga ended with their mass suicide in 1997.

This form of UFO-related cult behavior reached Sweden through the disturbing mind of "Mother Lilly,"" Lilly Gardeby. Her organization, World Light Center, was founded in 1983 and dissolved after her death in 2004.

She claimed to be the mother of Jesus and, through channeling, was in contact with everything from God to aliens. When journalists visited her in the '90s, she showed them two wooden barrels in her garden, supposedly cradles for alien babies! While her cult never descended into death, it still kept its members under strict, and sometimes very absurd, control. She came under scrutiny when she forced one child to eat their own vomit, which resulted in the involvement of the police. Many children got hurt, mentally and physically, over the years.

Before leaving the fascinating subject of Swedish contactees, I would like to bring up Sture and Turid Johansson, whom I mentioned earlier. A fascinating couple indeed, with their own harrowing experience—in parts both similar and very different from the one Ante had.

It all began in 1964 after attending a meeting with *Ifologiska Sällskapet*, the Ifologian Society. Active from 1957 to 1969 and based on the idea that Earth was visited by humanoid aliens from our solar system, the more rational-minded author (and once board member) and researcher K. Gösta Rehn described the society like this: "They have meetings that seem like prayer meetings. Many cultured ladies attend. Most are spiritualists, occultists, theosophists, telepathic believers, etc. So I am not in harmony with that clique. But we drink tea and discuss, and a lot of literature is available." Sounds fun.

Not long after Sture and Turid had visited one of their lectures, a strange thing happened. Turid was on the phone with a friend when a male (possibly inner) voice interrupted their conversation and said that she and Sture should go to Väggarö, south of Stockholm. They drove out to the designated location and started to meditate in their car, finding themselves surrounded by light-blue energy waves in their vehicle. Later that winter, they did it again, stepped out in the dark, and stood on the gravel road. Suddenly, a bright light came at them from behind, and thinking it was a car, they jumped down into the ditch, but could only see how the light moved straight up in the sky and disappeared.

One year later, on October 29, 1965, Turid received a mental message to once again visit the spot, but also with a warning, as "there is a power struggle on Earth." This eerie detail didn't stop the couple, and they drove out to their new favorite spot again, and this time they weren't alone. By the side of the road, and as close 30 meters to the car on Sture's side, a bunch of short beings were floating around. In an interview with Håkan Blomqvist in 1973, Sture recalled the episode: "When we arrived at the location where we were told to go, the usual place, something was already off. We were supposed to be there at 10.:30 p.m., but arrived at 9:30 p.m., and the beings were already there. We didn't see them until we parked the car, it was at dusk and not totally dark yet. They were down at the field and came up very close. I'm not sure how many there were, maybe five or six." Sture continued to describe the beings as short, approximately 125 to 150 centimeters with huge heads and glowing eyes, like red phosphorus.

Both were very scared and didn't dare to go outside as the beings were floating around them. Suddenly, their car radio started to make a terrible, high-pitched noise. When the car started to shake, the frightened couple took shelter in front of their seats, squeezing themselves in the cramped space. "We thought they would break the car!" Sture added.

The whole incident lasted for, they think, maybe five minutes. It was difficult to say, but it felt much longer. Somehow, time was lost, and they departed for home at around four that morning. The experience shook them to the core and forever changed their relation with the place. When Håkan Blomqvist interviewed them about the event, Turid described it as follows: "It's so weird, earlier when we went out there and experienced the lights, we never had a feeling of something sinister. We just had fun and meditated. But after this, with the beings, we just feel it's creepy out there. We won't even dare to go out when it's dark and especially not leaving the car!" The day after, they took a deep breath and visited the location again to look for traces but found nothing. One thing that might be worth noticing is that during the year leading up to the main incident, they repeatedly felt like someone was trying to stop them from going there. In Turid's words: "When we planned to go out meditating, the car kept breaking down. If it wasn't the light that didn't work, it was something else. It happened all the time, and it was as if we were prevented in every way from getting out that winter. Once the car stopped completely, it was impossible to get it going; neither lights nor anything worked. Then we thought, if we want something, nothing should stop us. We put on our boots and left. That's a lot of kilometers."

Looking at it now, their experience feels like a meeting with nature spirits: elves, fairies, etc. Or, as folklorist Dr. Simon Young calls them, landscape spirits. Their etheric appearance, the presence of strange blue lights in the area, and the short stature of the visitors remind me more of fairies or gnomes, and lack the physical presence in comparison to what Ante experienced.

Unlike Sture and Turid, Ante's experience resulted in him becoming a happier person, more relaxed and open to other people. But up until his death, he wasn't sure of what was really happening. "I still do not understand it today. Sometimes I go home and wonder if it's not just imagination or if someone lurks in me when I lie down and sleep. But I have accepted it for what it is, whether it is chimeras or reality," he told Clas Svahn in a 2014 interview.

One thing we know for sure: Ante never wanted to become a guru or a god to anyone out there. He just wanted to enjoy his happiness in peace.

eleven
like the wings of a dragonfly

IT WAS as if our oblong, curvy country was slowly adapting itself to the strangeness of the world in the 1980s. We'd had the flower power generation and the weirdness of the 1970s, which quickly transformed into paranoia and cynicism. People wanted joy, happiness, and hope for the future, and at the stroke of midnight on the night of 1980, I bet hopes were high. It didn't last long.

Maybe the "land of sin" lost its innocence with the assassination of Prime Minister Olof Palme and the Chernobyl disaster in 1986? The almost childish melodrama of political intrigue and the dangers of radioactivity clouded our minds, even as the Cold War slowly warmed up. However, in that green, lush Swedish countryside, there was still a certain calmness before the storm.

As a child during this time, the only thing I remember was the constant submarine incidents in the Stockholm archipelago. Since 1981, witnesses had seen and reported submarine activity in the idyllic waters outside the capital. There were weird sonars, mysterious bubbles, a sneaky periscope or two, and underwater vehicles had left strange tracks on the seafloor—and maybe there was even a blurry photo or two of some kind of craft poking up its metallic appendix from the watery, murky depths outside beaches crowded with sweaty, suntanned families.

Very few were aware of it at the time, but the similarity between the submarine hysteria and the ghost fliers of 1937 and the ghost rockets of 1946 was remarkable. There were thousands of reports regarding mysterious flying objects, secret military spy planes, or other technology invading both our skies and our newspapers. The submarine craze was the same, just underwater. Was it all hysteria, or was there any truth underneath it all? In 2022, we once again had a rash of reports, this time of unidentified drones buzzing around nuclear power stations and other locations of interest for national security.

All of these flaps were somehow related to alleged threats—tangible stuff, and foremost, something that everyone could understand. A safe spot in a sea of chaos, a blame-the-others anchor. Suddenly, everyone became a victim-by-proxy because THEIR country had been invaded by evil Russian killer submarines!

As a young boy, I always loved to hear about weird stuff, you know, in the same vein of strangeness—but with a dash of otherworldly entertainment. The submarine mystery was totally up my alley. What was out there? One thing that didn't reach the news at the time was the utterly strange incident that happened in the south of Sweden, outside the small community of Årnäs. It's an incident that I would have loved to read about as a kid.

Ulrika Åberg and Jörgen Berg, a young couple in their mid-twenties, had just gotten into their Ford Taunus and were leaving the tiny village of Årnäs for their newly acquired home in Mariestad. The year was probably 1985.

The clock had just struck 10 p.m., and they were eager to get home and cuddle up in bed after visiting Ulrika's parents in Årnäs. It had been a long day, but the drive home would only take them less than half an hour. To their left, behind the picturesque farms and fields, Vänern, the biggest lake in Sweden, was hiding. It actually has its own sea monster, Koffa, described as a serpent-style creature of three to five meters in length. Some stories depict it as a sinister entity luring fishermen down into the dark abyss. The latter is not unlike the Skogsrå, the forest nymph, a woman stealing the souls—and maybe lives—from lustful hikers and lumberjacks.

But that's another story. Let's get back up on dry ground again and the further adventures of Ulrika and Jörgen.

The couple had just passed the old convenience store and entered a long stretch of asphalt road with thick forest on both sides. Ulrika sat in the front passenger seat while Jörgen was driving. The only thing they could see was the road being lit up by the headlights, until something strange appeared in front of them.

They saw it at the same time, but from slightly different angles depending on their positions in the car: a weird, almost ethereal "thing" hanging by itself over the road. From Jörgen's point of view, he saw a ball—a big sphere, grayish in color—that looked like one of those pieces you play with in the Fia med knuff board game. There was a cone on top of the ball, partly inserted into it with the tip down. The ball wasn't reflecting the headlights; instead, it seemed to absorb the light, creating a gray void. It felt unreal. Attached to the ball and the cone was a stem—a long, thick string approximately centimeters in width—which went right up into the air.

From Ulrika's point of view, she couldn't see the ball but instead focused on the stem itself and what was above it. The stem, according to her, had an orange and brown glow emanating from it. It was burning with orange-brown colors. When the light from the car hit it, it seemed to get trapped inside it, "like a cloud" was Ulrika described it.

What really drew her attention, though, was what seemingly kept the thing up—a pair of wings, like the wings of a dragonfly. At least, that's the closest she could describe them.

Moments later, stunned by what they were seeing, the car silently hit the ball and the stem. The stem itself acted a bit like rubber as it bounced over the car. They passed the object and continued forward as if nothing had happened. They talked a bit about it, but their numb reaction to the incident surprised even themselves afterwards. It was like it was too strange to even comprehend. They had never seen anything like it and had no idea how to process this.

How to define this incident? It is an unidentified flying object, a UFO, for sure, but lacks all the typical trademarks of what one would usually expect from such an observation. If looking at it as some kind of alien object, was it an extraterrestrial spy drone? Maybe a so-called von Neumann probe—a self-replicating spacecraft—a theory put forth by the German mathematician John von Neumann:

"Von Neumann proved that the most effective way of performing large-scale mining operations such as mining an entire moon or asteroid belt would be by self-replicating spacecraft, taking advantage of their exponential growth. In theory, a self-replicating spacecraft could be sent to a neighboring planetary system, where it would seek out raw materials (extracted from asteroids, moons, gas giants, etc.) to create replicas of itself. These replicas would then be sent out to other planetary systems. The original 'parent'' probe could then pursue its primary purpose within the star system" (Wikipedia).

Perhaps it was a boring thing, like a human-made balloon with a weird design, on the run from its owner? It might have been, but there's never been an answer to this. No one has ever claimed to own such a thing, and nothing has been found looking like it. Remember, this was in the mid-eighties, and the drones of today weren't available at the time. Ulrika and Jörgen still have no idea what it was, and the later investigation and interview done with Swedish researcher, author, and ufologist Clas Svahn hasn't given any answers.

So let's go wild—none of us have anything to lose here. Let's get rid of the most logical explanations: a balloon or a hoax of some kind. Let's venture further into the wilderness of speculations—not, admittedly, very scientific or even rational; the latter has never been my strong suit. I prefer the wild, wild world of imagination.

Two things come to mind, at least for me, when researching this: some kind of insect cryptid. Let's call it—in the words of John A. Keel—an ultraterrestrial, an entity so weird it lacks any comparison in our known nature, an insect or other kind of animal not known to man, phasing in and out of our reality through dimensional rifts.

"Oh, he's crazy," you say? Yeah, maybe. Just live with it.

The other explanation is that Jörgen and Ulrika encountered some kind of alien species. We seem forever trapped in the idea that aliens, from space or another dimension, would look like a classic gray: small in stature, big head, black eyes, and thin limbs grasping after unsuspecting victims in their beds or tumbling out of a newly landed flying saucer on some deserted desert strip. Much of this we can blame on Whitley Strieber's (to be fair, very intriguing) book *Communion*, where the poor author is terrorized by very freaky beings from other worlds. A case of extreme lucid dreaming, the delusions of a madman, the cynical writings of a commercial author—or some kind of reality? We might never know. One thing is for sure, that cover scared the crap out of me as a kid.

Is this the only report of its kind in Sweden? Yeah, at least when it comes to something of this shape and behavior, but there have been other organic-looking objects flying—and swimming—around in our part of the neighborhood.

In 1981, Nils Berg and three other people were out walking in Uddevalla. When looking up at the sky, they suddenly saw an object shaped like a flatfish, approximately one hundred meters up in the air. Underneath were red pulsating lights, and a low thunder was heard. The object was seen by five other people along its flight path. According to the Swedish Air Force, they had no plane up in the area during that time.

Another flying fish was seen by farmer Svante Riekkola on January 29, 1971. Svante and his parents were on the road between Muodoslompolo and Pajala, on the border between Finland and Sweden. Looking up, they noticed a bright object shaped like a fish coming down from the sky with bouncing movements. It stopped fifty meters from the car, four meters above ground, and then took off and disappeared. The fish-shaped object was also seen in two villages, Kihlangi and Aareavaara.

In 1980, on August 24, a man in Strömstad was sitting and relaxing on his balcony with binoculars when he saw an object, shaped like a stingray fish, fly past him at a level of two to three hundred meters. As an experienced pilot himself, he claimed it was going at least 200 km/h. It was silver on the top and red and blue at the bottom, making wiggling movements. Even in this case, the Swedish Air Force denied having any vehicle in the area.

One of the oddest stories I've heard, but I'm afraid I can't confirm the authenticity of it, is pure hearsay. I'd like to share it for the sake of getting it in print. A colleague of mine mentioned that a former, quite famous comedian and TV host, many years ago was on his way home from a party. It was late at night, and he took a shortcut over a field. When looking up, he saw what he described as a giant stingray moving over him with slow, soft movements, just like it was swimming underwater—but up in the air. This is all I know about this, so I'll leave it for now. Maybe one day I'll get an opportunity to revisit this incident, hopefully with more details.

On a different part of the spectrum, which ties in a bit to the later submarine craze in the Stockholm archipelago, we find eleven-year-old Ove Olsson who, in 1978 on the evening of October 11, witnessed something very odd in the stream going through Torshälla. When walking by the water, just behind the local food establishment Krusgården, he saw movement in the water. In front of him, eighteen to twenty brightly lit objects were swimming around, all the size of soccer balls. Sometimes they peeked up above the surface, but mostly kept underneath. In a flash, almost like they seemed to have noticed the boy, all but one of them changed direction and swam away towards the archipelago. Ove threw a stone at the remaining object, which, like the others, had some kind of buzzing noise, but it just moved slightly and stayed in its spot. He quickly ran home to tell his friends and father about what he saw. They all ended up seeing the object. After tossing one final stone at the strange submerged visitor, it started to move and scurried away in the same direction as its buddies.

When it comes to cases with oddly shaped objects in the sky, the observation Siw Fester during the night of August 21, 1983, stands out as extra creepy.

Siw woke up at 2:05 a.m. in the morning with an urge to drink water. She noticed a bright light outside her window, and when taking a look, she saw a big object hovering approximately 10 meters above the ground, 120 meters from her house. It had the shape of a plate. After observing it for no less than twenty-five minutes, something happened that shocked her: twelve to fifteen long legs came out from the sides and slithered down towards the ground. It looked like a big, scary spider floating in the air, with the sound of bumblebees coming from it. It was spinning, doing one round in about three seconds. The legs straightened out, and the object landed in an opening in the nearby forest. The next day, a few neighbors joined her at the landing spot and found a circular mark in the grass, eight meters in diameter. The grass was burned and pushed down from a considerable weight.

Nowadays there is often a logic in the design of aliens and UFOs. It feels like the eyes are in the right place, and the craft are shaped to fly smoothly through the air. Most of mankind needs logic to grab ahold of things with—a comfortable familiarity in biological and technical design. But the universe, the ultradimensional and the physical worlds are so much larger than that. There must be—and I say this as a very unscientific person—a wide array of life forms and craft designs out there, all with their own unique environments to adapt to.

In the incident observed by Ulrika and Jörgen, the question

arises if such a flying ball/alien drone/dragonfly-winged ultraterrestrial entity would even be able to work or survive on our planet? Maybe it was just a reflection of another world, suddenly appearing and disappearing in front of the young couple? A shadow leaking through from somewhere else?

They are now in their late fifties and early sixties and are still living in Mariestad, now operating a mechanical workshop, constructing and producing tools and machines for the manufacturing industry. When I reached them on the phone during 2022, I was met by a loving, curious couple who told the exact same story as in the original report. Nothing has changed—and they still have no idea what they encountered that night outside Årnäs.

The mystery lives on, and I sense they both appreciate that odd piece of the puzzle they encountered many years ago.

twelve
owls and ufos

THE FIRST TIME I became truly aware of the connection between UFOs and owls was when I saw Olatunde Osunsanmi's *The Fourth Kind* (2009). Milla Jovovich plays psychologist Dr. Abigail Tyler, who moves to the small, desolate town of Nome, Alaska. She soon discovers a disturbing pattern between strange dreamlike experiences the locals have involving owls. Constructed as a mix between drama and documentary, the story unfolds chilling revelations between mysterious disappearances and UFOs —yes, good old alien abductions.

The film caused controversy when it came out, both from those who were initially fooled by the claim that it's based on true events and filmed regression therapy sessions (something that Jovovich herself states in the introduction to the film), and the citizens of Nome who got angry because they felt it was capitalizing on real disappearances in the area. Between 1960 and 2004, no less than twenty-four people had disappeared there, and the rumor mill was running wild. Was there a serial killer on the loose? Maybe aliens and their always present flying saucers were the culprits of these gruesome events? No bodies were ever found. According to the FBI's investigation, the disappearances were the result of excessive alcohol consumption in combination with the harsh winter climate.

It might seem a bit tasteless to make a movie about it, at least that's what Nome thought, but *The Fourth Kind* is still—after all —a pretty good chiller. And it introduced owls to a mainstream audience in a very intriguing way.

The owl connection to UFOs and high strangeness wasn't new at the time. The bird was mentioned most famously in Whitley Strieber's book *Communion*, where the author tells the fascinating story of his own possible abduction and contact with beings from another realm: "There was a white owl that used to stand in our backyard and watch the windows of my bedroom when I was a child. It made my folks nervous. This was during the time that they started nailing the screens shut." Strieber also mentions how, the morning after his first encounter on December 27, 1985, he woke up with a very strong discomfortable feeling and the intensive memory of having seen a barn owl looking at him through the window. Very creepy if you ask me. I won't bring up the history of UFOs and owls here—there are others who have already done it better, for example Mike Mclelland in his book *The Messengers: Owls, Synchronicity and the UFO Abductee*, and its sequel, Stories from *The Messengers: Accounts of Owls, UFOs, and a Deeper Reality*. Instead, I will look a bit closer at a few cases where owls have played a part in Swedish cases.

Like so many other teenagers during the summer of 1966, our two witnesses—two fifteen-year-old boys—had been out enjoying themselves and were now on their way home. Söderbärkeparken, situated eight kilometers from their home in Sörbo, Dalarna County, was—and still is—a very traditional Swedish peoples park,"" a venue where dances, concerts, and markets are held. And also, at least once upon a time, a popular hangout for youths. At Söderbärkeparken, or "Pärlan vid Barken" (the pearl by Barken—which is the name of the nearby lake—as it's called), an octagon-shaped dance floor and stage was the central point, often hosting a pop band or other kind of artist. The boys shared one moped this evening, modified of course—and therefore illegal—and took the smaller dirt roads home to avoid getting caught. It was a Saturday in July, and life was fab.

Around halfway home, it was time for a pee break. While standing there, one of them suddenly saw an owl up on a hayrack, looking down at them. It was dark, but the kind of summer darkness you can only experience in Sweden: bright and perfectly visible. The main witness, who much later, in 2009, reported the incident, was an avid bird watcher and wanted to show the owl to his friend. He aimed the moped's headlight towards the owl, and through that revealed something way more bizarre hidden in the darkness.

At a height of one to two hundred meters, and on a forty-five-degree angle from where they stood, a huge, silver-colored craft was hanging silently in the air. It was a matte metallic and moving very slowly, while at the same time flashing like camera flashes. The size of it was impossible to tell, but the witness describes it as a horizontal high-rise with some kind of clear, visible structure. They decided to follow the strange craft as it moved slowly over the countryside until it seemed to land in a field. The latter is difficult to tell, as a mist was surrounding it—the only mist during this clear summer night. After hovering over the field for a while, it took off again and seemed to be moving along the power lines.

Excited by the strange sight, they decided to quickly drive home to tell their parents. As they did, with around three kilometers left, the craft flew away with powerful speed until it was merely a bright dot in the sky.

It seems that the owl was the start of it all, a messenger of some sort. At least, if you want to see the experience as something out of the ordinary, which it certainly was for the teenage boys. Seeing owls as an omen of something supernatural happening is common and further connects the animal—as a symbol or physical being—to the phenomenon in a fascinating way.

During my research, mostly with the help of old Swedish UFO magazines and newsletters, I have found several incidents where the witnesses were outdoors for the sole reason of specifically seeing or hearing owls. The owls weren't present before, during, or after the incidents—or even considered important—but the purpose was to find them. In one case in the UK, the well-known researcher Jenny Randles found out that what the witnesses saw was an owl. It was flying at night, holding rotten fluorescent mushrooms in its beak, causing an observation of something that at first seemed out of this world.

In a letter to *Galaxen* in 1998, the membership magazine for the Umeå UFO Association, an unnamed woman described a very odd—and otherworldly encounter. She and a friend were out bicycling one evening in October 1993 when she noticed the beautiful aurora borealis covering the sky. Looking up, she saw what she first thought was an airplane coming towards them. However, it wasn't a normal airplane, as her warning to her friend reveals: "It's a monster airplane! A monster airplane!" she yelled in panic.

The front of the craft was elongated with protruding nails, and on top, domes were visible. It didn't become any less scary after it flew down, up close (no less than ten meters away!), and hovered in front of them, with the nails pointing towards her, which made her think she would be impaled. It then slowly turned until they could see the side where a big window or opening became visible. Out came a white-gray-like alien with big black eyes and visible pupils. It smiled at them with its thin, lipless mouth.

It wasn't until afterwards, after the craft had taken off and she was home, that she started to remember more details from the encounter. She had met two other beings, not counting the smiling one exiting the craft at the start. One was a terribly ugly turtle-like creature with pitch-black eyes. She was so scared of it that she didn't dare to talk. Instead, someone else took the lead, with a—in relation to this text—more familiar look.

It was very similar to a big owl, with feather-ish fur and three arms (!), and with no beak. The owl creature spoke telepathically with her and asked how humans lived and other general questions. It seemed like the turtle creature and its race were sick, and she noticed it looked sad.

This is a wild story—and one of those where one might wonder if it was all just a hallucination, vivid imagination run wild, or just an attention-craving hoax. The woman chose to be anonymous, which (kinda) removes the last one, but as we all know—the craving for attention comes in many different costumes. On the other side, it has that dreamlike quality I appreciate with encounters—a big owl with three arms? Why make up such a thing? Could this be seen as the shape-shifter archetype, a deformed way to show itself as something familiar to keep the witness calm? It feels much like an inner experience, with a net of symbols and past information/experiences coming together to a profound event for the witness. One might ask why these beings always come to our little planet to ask for advice and support? Is it our own inner wish to feel important that manifests itself through events like this?

Let's reconnect with the 1966 encounter with the owl as a messenger—or a portal—into another realm. In August 1980, the Swedish expat and Chicago citizen Ingvar Oskar Johansson was in Sweden on his yearly visit. He and his eleven-year-old son were driving from the Swedish east coast to an overnight stay in Åseda. It was late in the evening, and Ingvar pushed the speed limit up to 100 km/h. Slightly south of Blomstermåla, he noticed, while his son was asleep in the backseat, how the whole sky was lit up by a light blue glow. Suddenly, a big owl flew up in front of the car, against the windshield, and sat down, looking at him. "The face of the owl was uncannily human," he later told a journalist. It was screaming at him. He didn't know how long it lasted, but he got terribly scared. The owl flew away, and Ingvar and his son continued their journey, still driving fast along the country roads towards Åseda. The drive went on for a couple of miles until the next strange thing happened, this time slightly south of Kråksmåla on Road 125.

On the road, he could see something standing. Ingvar first thought it was a moose, but the closer he got, he noticed it was floating above the asphalt. It wasn't a moose. It was something more sinister and was slightly crooked, like it was hunched over a bit. The being was covered with brown-gray short fur, and it "stood" on two legs. Together with a tail and long ears, it had two distinct horns. "Ahead of me on the road stood the evil one himself. I'm no fool, and I don't believe in the devil, but I've seen him." The creature swept over the car, and he stopped to check that he hadn't hit someone. Nothing was to be found.

Once again, we're encountering the owl as a gatekeeper or an omen into the unknown, a sign that something is coming at you. Ingvar was a practical man and couldn't find any meaning or symbolism in his encounter. Today it's easy to see something else than the devil, namely the goatman. The legend of his horned beast was popularized in the early seventies when a family in Maryland blamed the decapitation of their dog on this creature, but the archetype itself, half-man and half-goat, could easily be seen as a modern faun or satyr of Greek mythology—or in this world of Hellier, the nature god himself, Pan. Why an atheist like Ingvar would encounter such a creature in the Swedish countryside is a good question, but he stood by his story for the rest of his life. This is, as far as I know, the only appearance of such a beast in Sweden.

Let's go back a few years, to 1947—a year that can be called the year of the UFOs. It was when Kenneth Arnold had his observation of nine flying objects above Mount Rainier—a sighting thatwhich, by mistake, coined the expression "flying saucer." A few weeks later, the infamous incident at Roswell caused headlines all over the world. The year before, in 1946, thousands of ghost rockets were seen above Sweden and the rest of Europe. Something was happening for sure, and maybe that's the reason Lieutenant Gustav Nilsson claimed he saw what he saw—an inspiring interpretation biased by the current news. Maybe he really saw something out of the ordinary? The thing is, it's just so damn odd.

Lt. Nilsson had been out on a military exercise at Mårtanberg, about fifteen kilometers outside the town of Rättvik, Dalarna County. It was him and his team, and they first noticed a hissing sound, like pressured air or steam being released, followed by two cigar-shaped objects flying at a distance of five to six hundred meters from them. Occasionally, the objects flew closer to the tops of the trees. On the front tip, they had something that reminded him of a car antenna. Lt. Nilsson grabbed a level and used it as binoculars, mostly to see if the objects had wings or not, as the witnesses discussed whether they could be gliders going down to land on a nearby field. The instrument was small and difficult to use, but he managed to write down a detailed description of what he saw: "The small windows appeared to be made in such a way that the whole body was painted on the inside. These round windows, however, appeared as lines all around. At the back, there were a large number of small holes or pipes that were directed straight back. A strange face appeared in the large window. It looked like a big owl head with big eyes but with a kind of mouth instead of a beak."

As the military man he was, he added that the owl face could have been some kind of mask or disguise. One thing was sure, it just wasn't painted to look like that. Captain Sund at the Defense Staff, later in 1952 (the same year as Lt. Nilsson reported the incident), was skeptical. How could the witness have seen all those details, more than referred to above, with just a level? No matter what happened that day in 1947, the result is one of the more odd observations from the era. Remains of the ghost rocket flap—or something else? Did Gustav Nilsson's eyes play a trick on him, or did he really see something out of the ordinary? We will, as you might understand, never know.

It's been tricky to find a connection between owls and UFOs in Sweden. Maybe it can be tracedbut take it with a grain of salt—to our detachment from nature, from what once connected us to the outdoors, deep forests, and fields. The owl is pushed out of our collective consciousness, as technology and "rational thinking" have taken over our old beliefs. I say a grain of salt because Sweden is literally covered with forests and other kinds of nature, and Swedes have a documented fondness for outdoor life. This doesn't mean owls are unimportant, and my stream of consciousness here might be contradictory. So be it. As Staffan Andersson brings up in his excellent book *Danaiderna: Ett försök att förstå UFO-fenomenet*, where he examines the relationship between Scandinavian folklore and UFOs, the owls have always been here. Vättar, mythological beings, were known to be shape-shifters and sometimes transform themselves into owls. The same with elves and other kinds of nature spirits. It's a symbol that comes back to haunt us, though twisted and absurd and injected with the modern UFO mythos.

A few years ago, my husband went out into the forest during nighttime to look for owls. He saw one sitting on the side of a tree, looking down at him. "Can you send me a feather?" he thought, and at the same moment, the owl let go of its grasp on the tree, flew over him, and down came a feather. A gift from Magonia, maybe? I choose to believe so. If someone asked me how to see a UFO, I'd say either go owl watching or fishing. Embrace the peaceful calm and remember to watch the skies.

thirteen
invitation to play

AS A YOUNG MAN, I lived in Jämtland, a county consisting of endless forests in all directions, crystal-clear lakes, and snowy mountains covering the border to our on-and-off friend, Norway. The area itself made my imagination run wild, especially with the everlasting Great Lake Monster swimming in Storsjön, next to the city of Östersund.

It was a place to contemplate oneself and explore life in a more physical way, such as skiing, snowmobiling, boating, or hiking. Considered an important spot for the Swedish military, the hills and grounds, and even some lakes, have hidden facilities. Many of them are now used for storage or, as in the case of those under lakes, flooded with water to stop people from getting themselves into trouble. It's a land of mystery and a perfect place for a young weirdo like me to dig deeper into the unknown. Looking out over Storsjön made me wonder many times what is really out there.

Once, while standing at the crossing between Brunflovägen and Bondegatan (this might have been in the end of the '90s), I saw a long, slithering object working its way against the currents down in the lake. It was twenty to twenty-five meters from head to tail. I observed it for a while until it disappeared out of sight. Maybe I saw the Great Lake Monster... or was it a figment of my imagination? Did I take part in the collective consciousness, the stories being told about a monster down in the deepest parts of the lake?

No matter what, it was a nice pause in what was a terrible period in my life.

One hour south of Östersund, you'll find Döviken, a part of Krångede. At the time, less than eighty people lived there—and now it's under fifty. A small community, to say the least. One of those people was Rune Asplund, a fifty-year-old train mechanic, living alone in his house. It was 9 p.m. on November 24, 1988, and, like many other middle-aged men in Sweden, he was enjoying a cup of coffee in the kitchen. Outside, the moonlight reflected on the snow-covered ground. Deep in his thoughts, perhaps contemplating life in general, he gave another glance through the window and saw, to his surprise, a very creepy scene not far from where he was sitting.

Around six meters away, a strange humanoid was standing. The body, as tall as a grown man, was glowing, shining, and dressed in a tight silver-colored overall. No face was visible. It could have been some kind of protection covering it. The clothes seemed to have been made in one piece; no seams were visible.

"What is this?" he thought, and continued to study the strange apparition for almost half a minute. The being stood with its arms out, like it was attached to a cross, and with its legs wide apart. It was rocking sideways, slowly back and forth. Rune, more perplexed than ever, got up and watched the event taking place from the short end of his kitchen table. Something had to be done! The curiosity of Rune was more powerful than his fear. He went to the hallway, grabbed his jacket, and, at the same time, still kept his eyes on the strange visitor through the door window.

It was visible all the time until he opened the door... and it had disappeared! There was no trace whatsoever on the snowy ground. The only noise that was heard was his three dogs barking intensively, as they often did when visitors came. This wasn't the first time odd things had happened at his home.

The year before, during the winter of 1987, his neighbor and friend Mikael Nilsson came for a visit. Mikael was a lumberjack and a practical, down-to-earth man. Like Rune, a man who was familiar with nature and the countryside. Much like the later incident, this observation took place in the kitchen, where the men sat and drank coffee at the table somewhere between 7 and 8 p.m. Mikael glanced through the window and saw, for a short moment, a small humanlike figure beside a footbridge. It was around sixty centimeters tall and disappeared before he could tell Rune about what he saw. They went outside to examine the grounds but found no trace in the snow of the mysterious visitor.

Stories of humanoids have been a tradition in Sweden since way back. Fairies, gnomes, elves, trolls, and other kinds of forest beings are part of our culture. We put all these critters under one umbrella, as "småfolk"—the little people. While the stories have faded a bit during modern times, they're still around and alive—but far more rare than those of UFOs and ghosts.

Let me tell you a story, and it's connected to the very existence of yours truly. It might be a long shot, but this is the story of how my family came to be, or at least a part of it.

My father's grandmother, Julia, was in her early twenties when she first arrived in Fagersta, in Västmanland county. It was in November, 1920, and she came by train to begin her new job as a maid for the postmaster and his family.

His house was situated a few kilometers outside Fagersta at Fagersta Bruk. Her new employer had ordered a horse-drawn carriage to come and pick her up at the train station. She waited patiently, but the driver didn't show up. There was either a misunderstanding regarding the time, or he had missed her somehow. Julia, even at the time a tough young lady, didn't let this bring her down, and she took her belongings, asked for directions, and started to walk.

It wasn't long after she saw someone in front of her, a small grayish being—a sprite, an elf, or fairy, whatever you want to call it—waving to her. She called it a "tomte," which in Sweden can be described as a small, bearded man with a pointy hat—like a typical gnome. It kept going forward, and she decided (yeah, she was tough) to follow it to wherever it might lead her. They walked (the gnome actually ran, because it had shorter legs) for quite some time until they came to a large house, where the little critter ran into the yard and disappeared. She knew directly this was the place she was meant to go to—the house belonging to the postmaster.

Moments later, a young driver with his horse and carriage came hurrying down the road and into the yard. He made excuses for the misunderstanding and that he'd missed picking her up at the station. He was obviously a young, sexy driver because they ended up falling in love and later spawning my father's side of the family. And here I am, whether you like it or not...

Stories of these small men come from all parts of Sweden. One of the more recurring places for observations was along the Kalix River. During the late 1960s and early 1970s, many people saw a small man appearing and disappearing mysteriously, often by the side of the road. The weirdest report might be the one Åke Westerberg experienced on the evening of February 16, 1971, when he was waiting for the bus. Up on a snowbank, he saw a small man with a square box attached to his belly. At first, he didn't notice anything strange and actually thought it was a friend. When he was twenty meters from the figure, it turned on an intensive light emanating from the box, so strong Åke had to turn away and cover his face. After a few seconds, the light went off, and the figure was gone.

At Skarvberget, north of Gävle, there were accidents involving cars attributed to trolls, elves, and other kinds of forest beings. The number of incidents was so high during a certain period that the location caused headlines all over Sweden. During the 1987 construction of the European route E4, protests from the nearby population were mainly focused on the danger of disturbing the otherworldly critters living in the area. Since then, the stretch of road has experienced deaths, electrical interferences in cars, flat tires, and other kinds of accidents. Rumors say the Swedish Transport Administration is covering up the number of accidents, which they deny—but admit that there have been more incidents there compared to other parts of the route. Not necessarily because of gnomes and fairies, though. Some stretches of road just have more accidents than others.

Let's continue a bit more with Swedish folklore before going back to Rune and his glowing humanoid. In the daily newspaper *Norrköpings Tidningar*, August 22, 1946, there's an interesting story about Lyktgubben, the Lantern Man. It's an apparition carrying a lantern or emanating an eerie light from its body, similar to the international stories of Jack O'Lantern and the will-o'-the-wisp.

Mysterious events have recently put a whole island in the outer archipelago outside Karlshamn in fear. Almost the entire population of the island has at different times observed a huge figure walking by the water, equipped with an old-fashioned lantern. The mysterious figure has put fear in the population. Fisherman Karl Berndtsson says the following to the newspapers:

"When we were approaching Tärnö with our boat from the south side, we suddenly saw the mysterious lantern-bearer. It was a dark night in August at around 11 o'clock, but the new moon shone so much that we could see the outline of the beach and the old trees, which go right down to the water's edge. Inside the Surviken Bay where the ghosts are seen, the water was still, and along the beach, a man, or whatever we shall call the mysterious creature, walked. It was a huge figure that seemed very impressive, even though he was hunchbacked and with his head against his chest. In his left hand, he carried one of those old-fashioned lanterns, and it shone with a strong fire-red light. The light flickered slightly and reminded me of an ember. We were only about 30 meters from the beach, and the man must have seen us, but took absolutely no notice of us. He went undisturbed at the same slow pace along the bay. After a while, he turned up into the forest and soon disappeared among the tree trunks. Why didn't we row to shore and pursue the lantern-bearer? Well, it sounds simple enough to say so in daylight. If I should be totally honest, none of us in the boat dared it, even though my friends and I are men of our best age and have been through a lot on the ocean. You may laugh about it if you wish, but it felt as if the creature radiated cold. Personally, I was freezing, and my mates also had malaise. I should mention that all three of us abstain from alcohol." There are many people on Tärnö who can tell you about the mystery. A sharp, perfectly normal young man in his twenties says that at a meeting with the mysterious lantern-bearer, he got such a strong shock he fainted for the first time in his life. "It was not the sight that scared me," said the young man, "but some kind of unexplained eerie impulse that emanated from the place where the red light was."

Surviken, where the mysterious lantern-bearer with the red light is seen most times, is a rather gloomy seashore. There is also semi-darkness in the middle of the day, and though there is much green, juicy grass, the island's many red-speckled cows avoid the site, even though they otherwise walk freely around the whole island. The lantern-bearer has appeared for a long time and been seen many times, but until now none outside of Tärnö had knowledge of the facts. Some twenty men and women, both young and old, bear witness to the phenomenon seen both from the sea and from the land side.

The lone figure, lurking in the night and carrying some kind of light, is well-grounded in folklore all over the world. What Rune saw feels like an update of that lore, but instead of a ghostly figure carrying a lantern, an alleged alien humanoid with a glowing appearance makes a visit.

Personally, I feel that Rune's experience is more related to Swedish folklore than UFOs and aliens, even if the silver man at first might seem more like a crab-walking extraterrestrial than a local gnome. The childish behavior of its movement might indicate that there was someone who wanted to have a bit of fun with

Rune out there in the darkness, a teenager eager for mischief wearing his snowmobile overall or some other kind of prankster.

And yes, it's hard to deny it might be related to the trickster element of the phenomenon. It seems like an invitation to play with the witnesses, like mischievous children, but the language is not understood—and when they don't receive the proper feedback, they disappear. It's like a game of hide-and-seek or tag on an otherworldly level.

Abductee researcher and artist (and admittedly quite problematic) Budd Hopkins mentioned that the abductees he worked with were often subjected to the presentation of a child, sometimes human and sometimes a hybrid between human and alien. Is this a hint to the controversial idea of hybridization, a symbolic way of connecting to the abductee, or, as some say, the result of leading questions from Hopkins himself?

Folklorist Thomas E. Bullard studied three hundred abduction reports and couldn't find any correlation between child presentations in abductions before Hopkins and his fellow colleagues started their research. He states that when people claim they have been abducted by aliens, children are often depicted as being examined or treated by the aliens. This may be because people think children are more vulnerable and in need of protection, which makes others feel empathy for them. However, the way people describe these experiences might be influenced by cultural expectations and biases, as well as other factors such as media exposure. Is the relatively modern trend of child presentations in abduction scenarios symbols of the abductees' vulnerability, created by the input from the hypnotherapists and researchers themselves?

There have been cases where witnesses have described the humanoids as children or childlike in their behavior. From what I know, it could have been children, but the connection to the otherworldly in the perception of the witness is interesting. Because kids, they're aliens of some sort. Not just in appearance with their big heads and oddly shaped bodies—but in how they walk, react, respond, think, and many other things. And sometimes, as scary or creepy as something unknown. They're strangers in our world, here to learn—or to pull pranks on unsuspecting adults.

Children want other children to play with. Is the childish behavior, the trickster persona of the UFO phenomenon, a projection of humanity's own lack of playfulness—or longing for it? John E. L. Tenney said that what the phenomenon wants is for us to go out and play, and maybe that's the invitation Rune and many others were given during their experiences.

Before we end this chapter, I would like to include another observation, not that different from the one Rune had but far away from the more common countryside. The place is a residential area in Skara, July 1, 2013. The witness is on his way to work by bicycle. It's around 6:45 a.m., and our hero, who will soon get the shock of his life, slows down a bit so he won't be too early to his workplace. One of his colleagues has the key, and he doesn't want to wait outside.

As he turns right onto a smaller path, he looks up and sees someone standing there, a someone that clearly doesn't belong in our objective reality: a weird-looking humanoid, around two meters tall with wide shoulders, no ears, no nose, and totally bald! With its bowl-shaped shoes dragging against the ground and its arms hanging straight along the body, it seems to walk directly towards the shocked cyclist! The closer it gets, the more details appear: a pear-shaped head, reminding him of that of a baby. The mouth is a thin line consisting of—what he could see—tiny holes. When passing the being, at the closest two meters away, he sees the eyes—rectangular in shape, with yellow irises and black pupils. They follow his movements slowly.

Our anonymous witness gets scared, which is understandable, but does not sense any threat from the strange visitor and continues on his bike. When looking back, he sees how the humanoid has stopped and looks at him and slowly becomes transparent and disappears. "I've read how people saw angels in the past, and I wonder if this was something similar?" he tells UFO-Sverige's Anders Berglund and Tage Bång in an interview for *UFO-Aktuellt* in 2017. They must have been strange angels if you ask me, but not so strange considering the accurate and nightmarish descriptions of angels mentioned in the Bible.

I'm not the debunking kind of person, and I totally respect the experience. He stood by what he saw and thought this was clearly out of the ordinary—even if he felt scared and never took the same road again after this incident.

The few times I've experienced something possibly paranormal myself, I've never felt scared or worried. The situation has often been so weird and unreal that I kind of detach myself from the absurdity of it, no matter if it was in Thailand, hearing the screams of an alleged nature spirit sounding like a crying baby, or seeing a compact, black shadow figure lurking three meters from me at a haunted old house. It was more a matter of observing the state of reality at the time than actually reacting to it.

I understand Rune's experience with the glowing humanoid. He sat there enjoying a cup of coffee, a luminous dude showed up at his house, and he just wanted to take a closer look. No drama, no fear. Just observation.

fourteen
what about that dead humanoid in sweden?

I'M A CURIOUS PERSON. Sometimes too curious. This curiosity often shows itself as me putting all my attention on nonsense. I hear or read something, a few lines here and there, even those in between. A word, a sentence uttered by someone—and I'm stuck. Is there a diagnosis for this? No, joking aside, my curiosity makes me healthy—but can also, if it leads nowhere, or me realizing how pointless it all is, lead me to the brink of depression. In this chapter I dive deep into a mysterious incident that somehow has gotten its own life in printed publications and on the internet, and for a while it completely took over my life and research.

Most of my free time between working on television projects and being panicked about being between jobs, I spend on reading books and magazines about flying saucers and humanoids. It's been a stronger and stronger obsession over the years. It began as a normal childhood interest, became more and more nonexistent for some years, until I had my usual edgelord conspiracy phase, which grew into boredom over the state of paranoia it just created—until I reached my current state of mind: old, vintage Swedish UFO and humanoid observations.

No, I haven't always believed in UFOs. Belief is the enemy, as

John A. Keel once wrote, and I hesitate to use that word even to describe my look at this subject. But let's say I'm interested in it, with a dash of understanding—based on all my research—that something is out there. What the heck it is, I have no idea, but it's there and it's fun. Through the years I've come to appreciate the hoaxers of UFO culture, those who during the early days manufactured made-up stories about otherworldly encounters to sell more magazines or get speaking gigs at UFO conferences. Or were they totally made up? Gray Barker is a good example, playing the role of Uncle Trickster in this subculture. A brilliant writer and a man who wanted to believe, but turned more and more bitter over the years.

In 1970, he wrote to John C. Sherwood, "The kooky books are about what I can sell these days..." as he found himself outdated by a new generation of ufologists—those who didn't appreciate his more or less speculative ideas and manufactured adventures of aliens humans. He might sound bitter, but it was because he was a believer—and he had reached the event horizon... and nothing more was to be discovered. What awaited him was another endless void.

In the chaotic field of ufology, tricksters and hoaxers are as important as serious researchers, contactees, and abductees, skeptics and debunkers. They're all part of the grand scheme, triggering each other into new discoveries, ideas, and failures. Gray Barker was one of the first who truly monetized his exaggerated vision of the visitors from outer space. In 1956, his book *They Knew Too Much About Flying Saucers* was published, the first book to deal with the Men in Black phenomenon. The publication spawned a whole new mythology, a mythology that somehow became a reality, at least if you choose to see it that way. Barker wrote and (in)directly manifested the MiBs, still present to this day—from witness statements to Hollywood blockbusters. Ray Palmer was another one. There's more, and we will get to more later in the text.

Personally, I always think of Robert Anton Wilson, who,

through his Illuminatus trilogy (co-written with Robert Shea), implanted the concept of the mysterious Illuminati society into the collective consciousness. Wilson himself was surprised when he was later contacted by representatives of his fictional organization, as they seemed directly connected to what he and Shea once wrote. Another example is when occultist and writer Alan Moore once met his own creation, John Constantine, in a bar. There are many more examples of this, the way imagination transitions into our reality. This form of thought-forms, manifestations, and tulpas fascinates me, and deep inside, I hope it will one day happen to me too, or at least something will show there is something tangible behind it all. Sometimes, stories take on a life of their own, like the following spectacular tale of a humanoid encounter.

"Dead Humanoid in Sweden." The four words stood out from the massive text I had just found. A dead humanoid in Sweden, an alien? I thought I knew about all the more spectacular cases of aliens, humanoids, and other kinds of monsters on Swedish soil, so I had to dive right into it! Could this be true, or was it just another creepypasta messing with my head? Like the earlier mentioned Halen vulture, the alleged pterodactyl at Lake Halen, and the Ällmora Swamp monster, for example, both probably creations of someone who was bored one day on the internet and decided to plant a few articles, forum posts, and comments here and there, creating two legends that only exist on the web and have no ground whatsoever in reality. To be fair, the Halen vulture was mentioned in a 1997 issue of *UFO-Aktuellt* and has been known since earlier. No matter what, was this another one of those stories?

I first found the story reported by cryptozoologist Brent Swancer under the full title "A Curious Case of a Dead Alien Humanoid in Sweden." After glancing through it, I had to find the source of this bizarre adventure! After using the internet for a while, I found a PDF file on Scribd credited to a Patrik Gross and something called URECAT—UFO Related Entities Catalog, described as "URECAT is a formal catalog of UFO-related entities sighting reports with the goal of providing quality information for accurate studies of the topic."

So, what's the story? What's this humanoid business? First of all, the case attracted me because it was set in Sweden, and I'm Swedish, and I research weird and strange UFO cases in this country. This one I had never heard about before, so imagine how my curiosity grew and grew... until the last notes in the PDF, written by Patrick Gross, where he kind of pulled the rug on the story. Maybe it was all fake? I'll get back to that a bit later. Now let's take a look at the story, as told by one of the three lumberjacks present at the scene, to a gentleman named John La Fontaine:

In 1955, three lumberjacks in Sweden saw a cigar-shaped object flying haphazardly in the forest before it crashed in a clearing. The crash caused a vacuum wave that sucked everything towards the center of the light, and the lumberjacks saw a lifeless body of a small, well-built man dressed in a reddish metal uniform with broad shoulders, yellowish skin, and black, deep-set eyes. The man's clothing appeared glued to his body, except for his head and hands, and his shoes had ribbed foot-soles that vibrated. The lumberjacks noticed a rectangular object with twelve small indents in the man's hand, and they saw the man engage the indents with a slate pencil before trying to throw it away, warning the lumberjacks not to touch it. The man spoke perfect Swedish and smiled reassuringly, revealing small teeth in the upper and lower parts of his mouth, with flat and broad canine teeth:

"The place I come from is in the vicinity of the constellation you call 'The Eagle.' Several races from space have visited your planet, some of them so far advanced that you could only see them when they materialized or dematerialized to visit a parallel universe in the orbit of Earth. Some of these visitors kept people on Earth under surveillance for thousands of years. Others took samples of the Earth with a view to later settlements. Still others have had contact with mankind for centuries."

According to the witness, the stranger gave him a folded bag from an invisible pocket just before he died, instructing the witness to put him in the bag and take him out to the river. The stranger explained that his body would disappear with the bag in the water, and the witness and two brothers were to rinse themselves thoroughly afterward to avoid getting ill. The stranger's halo gradually disappeared, and his buckle got darker as he took his last breaths. The witness heard the stranger speak in a language he didn't recognize, but then he spoke in Swedish, saying some final words, which the witness believed were a prayer to some deity.

The witness, with the help of the two brothers, carried the stranger's body in the bag to the river. The bag smelled of sulfur and burned their hands, and the water around it bubbled for a few minutes, suggesting a chemical reaction had occurred, before it was dissolved. The witness thought that maybe the stranger had hoped to die quickly in the river instead of suffering for a couple of hours before dying. The witness stayed with the brothers for a couple of years but rarely talked about the special day. He remembers it vividly, even though the brothers are now deceased.

Intriguing.

The source used is the tabloid magazine *UFO Universe*, specifically the August/September 1991 issue, which boasts headlines such as "BEWARE THE SINISTER GRAYS—THEY MAY BE OUT TO ABDUCT YOU," "UFO ABDUCTION HORROR," and "DID ANCIENT ASTRONAUTS BRING ELECTRICITY TO EARTH 2000 YEARS AGO?" The magazine also includes ads for Nina Nostradamus, who is claimed to have "predicted the 1989 San Francisco quake within eleven minutes," as well as books such as *Cosmic Top Secret* by William Hamilton III and *You Can Become A Super-Being*, complete with an "actual photo of a fire god created with the powers described in this new book." It's not all fun and games, of course; within its pages is a good article by English researcher Jenny Randles and several other more thought-through works. But I wanted to own this issue for the headline on the cover: "Alien Dies in Sweden."

The text is credited to one John La Fontaine and is riddled with sloppy facts. This didn't just make me suspicious; even Patrick Gross had a theory: John La Fontaine is an alias. According to Gross, *UFO Universe* was a supermarket tabloid, which is true, and therefore ran a lot of completely made-up stories just to sell more. The editor was the notorious Timothy Green Beckley, a trickster in ufology and conspiracy theories who balanced between fact and fiction, much like Gray Barker did. Gross also puts forth that John La Fontaine is a version of Jean de La Fontaine, a French author of fables, or so-called fabulist, who lived between 1621 and 1695. He wrote twelve books with 239 fables in total and was very popular at the time.

So Gross has a point here. The names are similar, and the story itself—with a Swedish-talking, short-statured humanoid crashing in the north of Sweden and then being dissolved like an effervescent tablet in a nearby river—is quite outrageous. It bears all the trademarks of a fable, a fairy tale. Living in Sweden, and with the more laid-back and mellow UFO culture we have here, I wasn't that familiar with Beckley and *UFO Universe* (and the tons of other publications he was behind), so I sent veteran occultist and ufologist Allen H. Greenfield a message on Twitter. If my memory serves me right, he had mentioned Beckley had been a friend of his. I asked him specifically if he knew if Beckley ever had used the name John La Fontaine, and got a very frank and to-the-point answer: "Not to my knowledge. Tim did publish stuff from an assortment of people with odd names, but his basic modus operandi was to print anything of interest that either wasn't nailed down by copyright or by his friends who didn't charge him. I knew him for nearly 60 years. He didn't have a mean bone in his body and was less cynical than Gray or Jim." (with Jim, Greenfield refers to his friend and ufologist James W. Moseley).

I trust Greenfield on this and decided to leave the subject of the dead humanoid in Sweden alone for a while. All my searches for John La Fontaine or John Fontaine in combination with

UFOs and humanoids only led me to rewritten versions of the article in *UFO Universe*. So maybe it was a dead-end street after all? But, like broken machines such as televisions, recorders, players, and so on, when you leave them alone for a while, they tend to work again after a shorter or longer break. It's a form of passive magic. So goes the universe. Just let it work out some things, and it will be there for you sooner or later.

It wasn't until I was bored one day and looking through Archives for the Unexplained's online database of scanned magazines and fanzines that I encountered something interesting. In issue six, 1977, of the Swedish magazine *UFO-Information*, I suddenly saw a very familiar but yet so modest headline: "Avled en man från en annan planet i Norrland år 1955?"—"Did a man from another planet pass away in Norrland in 1955?" signed by John La Fontaine. It was translated from Danish by Jan-Ove Sundberg, and the source was issue four of the Danish publication *UFO-Aspekt*, 1977. I finally found it, the source of the story, and it had been written down way earlier than 1991. The question still remained: Was John La Fontaine an alias? As for Beckley, he had been active during the seventies, but why would he write for a Danish publication?

What really made me happy was that the information in both the Swedish and Danish versions was finally correct. The main issue is the confusion over the actual location. In *UFO Universe*, it is said to have been in "Charlottenborg, Copenhagen, Sweden." First of all, as is well known, Copenhagen is in Denmark, but on the other side, there's a Charlottenberg in Sweden with a slight difference in spelling. This was solved quickly. The scene of La Fontaines encounter with the mysterious man had been at an exhibition called Love or Chaos at Charlottenborg, an art center in Copenhagen. There was no year stated, but using the Danish original name of the exhibition, Kærlighed og Kaos, I found out that there was actually an exhibition between April 15 and April 30 with that name in 1977.

Christiania is a free zone in Copenhagen created by hippies, free-spirited supporters, and a huge amount of hashish. When the Danish government decided to close down Christiania in 1976, the community appealed to the supreme court in 1977 and lost. One of the measures they took to keep Christiania going was the art exhibition Kærlighed og Kaos. It was a big success, and among the exhibitors was FUFOS—Frederiksbergs UFO Studiokreds and/or Frit UFO Studium. According to UFO Universe, the organization had members at its peak and was led by the charismatic channeler, psychic, and ufologist Steen Landsy. He has been a professional in the field since 1969 and has run Kosmos Center with his wife, Ingelise Landsy, since 1976. But the question still remains: who was or is—John La Fontaine? I sent Landsy an email to ask about the incident involving the dead humanoid and the author of the article. The answer didn't give me much, but at least I knew I was on the right track: "Unfortunately, I do not remember anything about the incident—but I can tell you that John La Fontaine was an employee-volunteer in the FUFOS association. Unfortunately, I do not know if he is still alive."

At least, I had confirmation that La Fontaine was a real person and had been active within FUFOS at the time. I headed to Facebook and became a member of the group Skandinavisk UFO Information – Debatforum," where one member told me that he remembered John La Fontaine very well since his teenage years. John had been a master of telling stories. Maybe being a former sailor was one of the reasons he knew so much about the world and UFOs. He was very active in FUFOS and traveled around Denmark to talk about the subject to the public. Sadly, he had passed away. Thanks to Thomas Michanek from UFO-Sverige, there is now a photo of La Fontaine. So I'd say that his existence is beyond proven.

As Fontaine had no means to capture the interview, neither by pen nor any electronic recording device, he fully admits that he wrote it down only from memory. At the end of the article in *UFO-Aspekt*, he calls out for the witness to contact him again so they can discuss it further. However, if the unknown man ever responded to him, it wasn't mentioned in *UFO-Aspekt*. Interestingly, someone else wrote to the magazine. While going through old issues of the magazine, Thomas Michanek found a short notice: a man claiming to be one of the brothers (obviously ignoring the statement that they died), and it was promised that this was going to be looked into. Whatever happened with that is unknown to this day.

The original witness, the man telling the story to John La Fontaine, had been in his sixties at the time of the encounter at the exhibition and must be dead by now. The few details in his story seem right but aren't specified enough to identify the exact location or the other two witnesses. It might all have been a hoax or the imagination of a man who needed some attention. What the truth is, we will never know, as everyone involved is either unknown or dead. This is what ufology is about, at least partly: storytelling, imagination, a delicate walk on the fine line between truth and fiction. Stories like this belong as much in the UFO culture as Tic Tacs, bright dots in the sky, contactees, abductees, field investigators, and boring, office-bound researchers like me. It's another trigger into the realm of the unknown and the curious concept of "what if...".

Swedish researcher and author Håkan Blomqvist has another theory, which he shared—or at least hinted at—in a recent email. "A certain parallel can be drawn to Albert Coe's book, *The Shocking Truth*," he wrote, attaching a PDF version of the book.

Albert Coe's book is the alleged true story of Coe, who was in the wilderness for months when he encountered a humanoid who had been wounded in a crash. Coe helped him, and they became dear friends. The basic setup is actually quite similar to what the unknown man told La Fontaine in 1977: the wilderness, the wounded humanoid, the communication between the two—but then it differs drastically.

Where Coe's friend, Xretsim ("Mister X""), or Xret as Coe called him, survives and continues to have contact with him (they even go on a fishing trip together), and it's all a secret between them, the Swedish story ends with the humanoid dying in front of the man and his two logger colleagues and is then dissolved in a nearby river.

Could the man have read Coe's book and taken the initial premise from it? Maybe he read it and somehow, with the help of a vivid imagination, it became a real event in his own life? It's perfectly possible, but yet—we don't know.

This is as far as I can get with the story, but to paraphrase John La Fontaine himself at the end of the original article: "*Dette er højst interessant, og når/hvis du, ukendte vidne, læser dette, bedes du venligst kontakte mig, så att vi kan uddybe detta emne nærmere*, or as the translation reads: This is very interesting because when/if you, unknown witness, read this, please contact me so that we can elaborate on this topic further.

If you know anything about this story, or the unknown witness, don't hesitate to contact me.

fifteen
borderlands

IN THE EPISODE "OFÖRKLARLIGA MÖTEN" ("Unexplained Encounters") from February 9, 2018, of the Swedish podcast *Historier från Hälsingland*, a very strange tale is told. It's not related to UFOs and aliens, but still in the amazing realm of high strangeness. In short, it's a letter from a listener who tells a story of how he and a few of his friends in 2002 encountered a group of wildman-like men out in the wilderness in Ljusdal, Hälsingland. It's a creepy story, but after hearing it, and only relying on hearsay and references on the internet earlier, I've come to the boring conclusion that it's a typical creepypasta: a fictional tale written to seem like the real thing. It's just too well-written and detailed, as if the writer is acting out the adventure while describing it—adding pointless, almost poetic details to a carefully constructed build-up.

While there was no shortage of lies and delusions in the past, I still put my trust more in old-school accounts of the weird than in newer stuff, especially since the latter is so much more focused on being shared for the sake of being shared. That's one reason I'm focusing on old cases in this book and trying to always go back to the original sources—to avoid the always-present game of Chinese whispers, which has a tendency to show its ugly head sooner or later.

In Sweden, we call it "The Whispering Game," a more logical name for when you whisper words in a friend's ear, and your friend forwards the message to another friend—or enemy—and so on. Everyone is curious how the message sounds when it reaches the final ear, which often comes out as something completely different. A story without a confirmed or anonymous source might be spectacular and intriguing—but in the end, lacks meaning, as it's basically a form of fiction.

We all know that the true nature of a good story is to be shared, but in this day and age, there's a higher chance of encountering cynically manufactured stories. It's so easy to get them out to the public, which doesn't necessarily mean it's easier to get attention. Drowning in the noise of (dis)information is the most common death of a great story nowadays. All that noise makes those in the business of make-believe more eager to boost their stories with fake videos, manipulated photos, and anonymous sources and witnesses—all in the name of the ultimate attention, which is always painfully short.

This creates a need to produce more stories, more dramaturgically correct spectacles to grab the eyes, ears, and minds of those inhabiting the internet. The world gets oversaturated by weirdness to the degree that it stops being weird and just turns plain boring.

We need to look at the stories from the past, as their weirdness feels more organic, chaotic, and less measured. You know them: witness reports and sketches printed in old flying saucer magazines or maybe found between book covers where contactees share the latest heartwarming gossip from their Venusian friends, or pocket books from the '70s where one strange case after another is written down with little or no references to their origin.

During my research, I've encountered several Swedish stories where I've come to the conclusion that they might be internet hoaxes, like the Halen vulture, a pterodactyl roaming the small town of Olofström and the nearby Halen lake. Through the phone, I reached one of the elders in Olofström, veteran book antiquarian Johnny Karlsson. Amused by my stories of an alleged pterodactyl, he told me he wished they were true and added that he had never heard anything about flying monsters in his neighborhood before—and he was a seasoned guide of the area and the lake himself.

The Monster of Ällmora Swamp is another one, a year-round creature who comes up from the depths of a forest lake to drown (and maybe eat!) both those brave enough to walk on the ice during the winter and swimmers and boaters during the summer.

None of these legends are based on creepypasta. Not what I've found anyway, just odds and ends of information showing up on old homepages and forums. There's nothing of tangible value to be found. Which makes me suspect that someone, whoever that might be, once tried to plant these stories for fun or as a part of some kind of social experiment. If you're reading this, congratulations, they're now officially in print and will continue to spread, evolve, and maybe one day be manifested into our reality. Yay!

I'd say that where there's smoke, there is fire, and when you can't find a fire, there's no truth whatsoever in the stories being told. Which makes it a lot more interesting when you actually find a faint glow deep down somewhere, hidden in an old magazine or told as a personal experience. For example, the Halen might have some truth in it - —as fossils of winged dinosaurs have been found in the same part of Sweden, Blekinge. Maybe the story grew from those facts—and turned into local folklore and later online fiction? But then we have those wildmen I mentioned in the beginning of this chapter, in Ljusdal, 2002. Imagine my surprise when I found not one but two, on the surface, similar stories. But this time they're grounded in reality, with incidents that could be confirmed by witnesses, locations, and dates.

On February 27, 1977, reindeer herder Nils Tomas Labba took the snowmobile from his home in Soppero to locate his reindeer. It was a cold, clear, and crisp morning, and he took the path along the Lainio river until he came to Lake Pojjujaure. In the distance, he saw four people, dressed in brown clothes—possibly overalls—walking on the ice towards him where he was sitting on his vehicle. When the group noticed him, they turned left and completely disappeared into a vibrating, transparent cloud that flew up in the air. Of course, he couldn't believe his eyes, but found no trace of the group.

Another highly interesting story was told by one of the witnesses themselves in episode 117 of the podcast *Fiskekompisen* on November 9, 2020. Henrik Strömberg Croné and a friend, Ulrik, were out fishing at Övre Vitådalen at the end of August 2005. It was late at night when they met two silent, noncommunicative men dressed in old-fashioned clothes wandering in the darkness on a deserted road miles from civilization. None of them was dressed for the occasion, nor carrying any modern camping and/or fishing equipment, and dragging their feet along the ground. Henrik and Ulrik could see how the two men walked by at a distance of ten meters until they disappeared into the night again.

There's no reason to believe Henrik tells a made-up story. It's a bit too realistic to just be imagination, but creepy nonetheless. What I find interesting is how similar stories, both clearly made up and those based on reality, show up—like the opposite sides of the same coin, reflections of events in distorted mirrors of reality.

Is it our life that imitates imagination, or are the stories themselves pathways into new, stranger possibilities? Occultist and ufologist Allen H. Greenfield writes in his book *Saucers and Saucerers* on the subject of hoaxes, imagination, and reality: "The UFO phenomenon exists on the borderline between reality, or what we choose to recognize as reality, and imagination, or at least what we tend to consider imagination. It may be that such borderline areas of human consideration (and there are certainly others, from utopian ideals to surrealistic art, from religion to philosophy) which, in an ultimate sense, do not lend themselves to rational analysis."

Is there any difference at all between our waking and dream states? Perhaps it's all the same, phasing in and out—and from time to time, someone notices it? If there's a chance one can encounter the past, is there a way the future can reveal itself to us?

"In November 1927, my father and I were logging on the south side of Niilijänkänmaa. I sometimes used to skip school to do this, with my father's approval. It can already be said that it was in my own great interest to join. It was also a matter of snaring birds and hares, which I really liked. Every morning I was in the forest, I went around the hunting trail and emptied the snares. Sometimes I caught several grouse and an occasional hare. One cold evening under the moonlight, Father and I saw an inexplicable sight that it would be wrong not to share, for there is still much between heaven and earth that no one can explain. The felling was 3.5 km south of the village. The days were short, but that evening we worked in the moonlight for a long time. When we were on our way home, I saw a huge ship, about two hundred meters long, maybe more, cigar-shaped and more narrow towards the rear end. The color was yellowish, brass-colored metal. In the upper half, there were dark round holes that resembled windows. In the lower half towards the rear end, there was a large dark opening like a gate. From there came out several round things, like two coffee saucers put together. These things moved with incredible speed. The ship itself seemed to move slowly north. My father had already gone a long way before I caught up with him. I saw the ship all the time. But soon the tree line would obscure the ship. I shouted at my father, so he stopped. I pointed to the ship, which was now going in the same direction as us, so we had to look to the right. Father had time to see for a good while even the little things that flew near the big ship before they disappeared behind the forest to the north. He could hardly believe his eyes either. We both understood that this ship and these objects were not from our earth. When we got home, we told my mother what we had seen. She wondered a lot about what this could be. For her, it was never a question of just fantasies. Sometimes I tell my friends about the experience. Everyone just laughs. You just become ridiculed. Because of that, it fell into oblivion for both Father and me. It was not until the 1940s that newspapers began to write about flying saucers. Dad was still alive and heard about the flying saucers. 'Well, now others have seen little things too. But we have seen the big mother ship.' Although it is 45 years since we saw the strange airship, I still remember the event as if it had happened recently. During these years, I have spent many nights hunting in the wilderness and looking at the starry sky and have never again been privileged to see any mysterious objects in the firmament."

The letter to *Norrländska Socialdemokraten* was signed by a man identifying himself as Enor. He would have been around sixty years of age at the time of publication, on December 28, 1972. The letter was accompanied by a drawing illustrating the mother ship and flying saucers, dated twenty years earlier, in 1952. I don't know who Enor was (and trust me, I've tried to find out!), or if his story is true, but did he just make it up one day while being bored, or did his mind tell him it was real after watching a late-night sci-fi movie on television? Or did something really happen out there in the wilderness?

One thing is true, whatever happened—or didn't—made such a big impact on his life that he had to write it down and share it with the public. I mean, damn it, if the dating on the drawing is correct, it means the incident was of importance to him not only at the time of the event but even later, in 1952, and then finally, in 1972. An event that haunted him from his teenage years, a unique father-son experience, to say the least. Enor didn't make this up, not deliberately. I'm sure of it. He had an experience, something so profound he never let it go. Did he and his father encounter a huge UFO from another world, or is it just a dream transcending into reality over many years looking up at crystal-clear winter nights by the fire, a place for contemplation and wonder? Or did they, through a rift in time, get a glimpse of the future?

As I've mentioned earlier, the presence of infinite silence and open skies, far from big cities, traffic, and people in general, seems to be the path to experiencing—and maybe understanding—the phenomena. I believe the silence of the mind, the constant defragmentation of our way to experience reality, is important for the ability to see beyond the materialistic worldview. Well, it's more the perfect meeting of them both—the practical way of living away from stress and noise; a grounded form of existence in combination with the seeker archetype, the new ager to some—the magician to others. Vuk from the podcast *Tracing Owls* has spoken about the same concept many times, that many of these cases are set in liminal spaces, locations set between other, noisier and more crowded places such as country roads, moonlit fields, a lone cabin in the woods, and so on. Time and space stand still, and the silence is outstanding.

Vuk has this idea that these liminal spaces are gateways or passages between our objective reality and the archetypes of our collective unconscious. In the podcast *6 Degrees of John Keel*, he says, "Maybe monsters are Jungian archetypes that exist in a social unconsciousness, that are invoked whenever humans experience something they cannot fathom, what I'd say is a liminal space or an unknown frontier. Forests were unknown frontiers. You still had people afraid of going into the forest and constantly having to battle wolves and denizens, etc., that came from this very mystical place they do not understand. And then people reacted to the forest by invoking these images of fairies or monsters. But now that we are cutting down forests and covering them in concrete, that's our way of dominating the unknown. What we have now is the ocean and the skies. So now instead of seeing lights in the forests, we see them in the skies—because we have chased off these fairies and monsters into the sky." Since Whitley Strieber's book *Communion*, where he tells the remarkable and very twisted story of how powers out of this world made contact with him, the now classic gray alien design has become the most common style of archetypical entity—the result of a mass-market propaganda machine in the shape of book covers, movies, and storytelling.

With more communication, more intense information flow, and distractions projected through the lenses of our minds, we perceive aliens, humanoids, beings, entities, etc. as less imaginative, creative, and outside the box. Our consciousness has become mainstream, and instead of high strangeness like the Pascagoula humanoid, the Hopkinsville goblins, Sam the Sandown Clown, and the Flatwoods Monster, we have pop culture space bros that no longer challenge our imagination.

Researcher and investigator John E. L. Tenney writes in his essay collection *Theoretical Weirdo*, "I want something magical, something that makes technologically advanced aircraft as boring as it actually is in the overall scheme of things. I want people to get along and have fun doing it because if we don't all get along, then not all of us will be able to ride in those flying saucers, and that's no fun for anyone."

Is it an oversaturated society we're living in, flooded by information that affects our imagination? One might think that the more we have to choose from, the more creative we get—when it's the total opposite. There's nothing left for us to create. Does the constant noise deprive us of the magic? Is what we see a part of a projection of our internal experiences/expectations and part of the external unknown, which comes together as the so-called phenomenon? If the latter is a white canvas with a certain amount of texture, our consciousness is the color we throw at it to see what patterns will appear.

What's needed is not the stereotypical "open-minded" kind of person, but a mind that accepts existence without judgment. When there's silence, there's time to feel instead of think and respond rather than react. We let down our guard and connect to the liminal spaces of both our consciousness and our physical, objective reality. The "Me"" is gone, and something else takes its place.

Most of the content in this book has been written early in the morning when yesterday's distractions are gone, and I'm free from censoring myself. The calmness of the silence is the borderlands, the mythological Magonia, the conspiratorial underground base of Phil Schneider, Alan Moore's Ideaspace—all the inner and outer spaces where unknown forces question our consensus reality. It's where tricksters play their—and not our—games and where, as John A. Keel bluntly put it in *The Eighth Tower: on Ultraterrestrials and the Superspectrum*, "God may be a crackpot." Damon Knight wrote it differently, but not less eerie, in *Charles Fort: Prophet of the Unexplained*: "If there is a universal mind, must it be sane?"

Let me expand on that: if there is a universal mind, and we are part of it, that means it must be insane. Yeah, downright fucking crazy. For good and bad, because a sane mind is also a terribly unimaginative one.

The phenomenon is a six-armed ape, tripping balls on acid while throwing feces around, and those getting too close will get hit in the face. That's basically what I think it's all about: chaos. There lies the key to studying the phenomenon, keep your balance, and don't go too deep into the rabbit hole.

sixteen
the stigma within the stigma

BEHIND THE COUNTLESS reports of bright lights in the sky, vague black triangles flying in the distance, and mysterious glowing areas behind the treetops, there's an array of incidents that, in the name of sanity, never get as much attention. Is it a form of self-preservation at work here? Witnesses don't want to be subjected to mockery. The media sees it as a question of mental health and not newsworthy. And UFO researchers who want to be taken seriously focus on information that might not make them a laughing matter.

It's not always like this, of course, especially from those deeply interested in the UFO phenomenon. All the sources I've gone through while writing this book are open-minded, uncensored, and with a high acceptance for the extraordinary. Serious (at least most of the time) investigations are undertaken. Reports are written, and everything is recorded and written down to be read and analyzed over and over again.

But as with the abductees and contactees, there's always this notion of not being taken seriously. It's easier to write about less cheesy things: stories and incidents not involving weird creatures and monsters, with more modern and logically shaped craft, and where the psychic connection is less pronounced. With a discreet smirk, stories are told as if they aren't meant to be taken too seriously. I've been guilty of this myself a few times during my younger years, especially when I've told stories to someone who's already a bit skeptical. They've been tales about fools and not folks, as I've been compromising myself for the sake of keeping up an image.

Look at the state of modern ufology, with its focus on military witnesses, "ex-government" types with secrets they can't tell, "trained observers" (which seems to be everything from police officers, pilots, security guards—well, everyone with a uniform), and other kinds of so-called authority. What makes them authorities in something so absurd and unexplained as unidentified flying objects, I don't know. In many cases, they just use the acronym UAP (unidentified aerial phenomenon), and they come out of it relatively unscathed, thanks to the blessing of a relatively modern rebranding of a subject that once was very fringe.

The use of the label "trained observers" puzzles me because some of them have a tendency to pull the trigger without looking too carefully at what's in front of them. Some of them hide behind the always-illusory authority of titles, labels, and uniforms —it's a ufology costume ball!

By dressing up in new words and acronyms, suddenly promoted "official" spokespersons, often from the world of intelligence and mainstream journalism, present blurry videos that say nothing about the phenomenon. The idea of UFOs has transcended from the murky depths of weirdness to bureaucratic porn and relentless boredom.

The price of breaking free from the stigma has become the degeneration of imagination. At the time of writing this, an unscrupulous apparel company, SAUCER, has trademarked "Unidentified Aerial Phenomena" and its acronym "UAP," a decision that has actually unified all branches of ufology, from believers to debunkers, in a mutual rage towards this further monetization of the subject. Where money and business come in, imagination and creativity go out.

The imaginative mind of the UFO culture has always been what attracted me: the on-the-surface madness that, with a closer look, reveals human experiences, personal insights, and the importance of being who you are and not the title you carry. It's bravery to report what's not expected from an observation, to not censor oneself for the sake of seeming sane.

To keep it short: in the end, I respect plumber/chicken farmer Joe Simonton and his space pancakes a thousand times more than intelligence spooks and their "threat assessments."

But maybe that's just me? Am I the fool here? A fool in the company of such great minds and radical thinkers as John A. Keel, Jacques Vallée, David Moore, John E. L. Tenney, Colin Wilson, Allen H. Greenfield, and many others. There is no further comparison between them and me, except that we're looking beyond our shared reality with exceptions to find nothing and everything at the same time.

I don't know what's going on. I have no damn idea what the phenomenon is really about, and I'm grateful for that. That puts me in a situation where, as John A. Keel put it, belief is the enemy. Whether that's true or not, I'll leave it to the cult leaders. Truth is —for better or worse—highly subjective, and the only decent thing to do is not to flaunt our own truths as something that our co-inhabitants on this planet Earth shouldn't be subjected to. It only creates fragmentation, and fragmentation makes conflict blossom. And to be honest, do we need more of that?

One of the biggest mind fucks I've ever had was when first listening to Alan Moore's hypothesis about what he calls "Ideaspace," the inner reality—which can manifest itself outwardly through both our own personal and shared imagination. The creation of a concept, let's say the mythology of *Star Trek* or *Star Wars*, spreads through the minds of their fans who create an even larger, wider mythology that expands with every thought being thought and shared. It's a reality of its own, just existing through—

for example—fan fiction. What I create in my mind is real; it's just not physical in the way I'm used to. It takes on a life of its own when mixed with the imagination of others. Ideas are explored, worked with, debated, put aside, embraced, or dealt with in any other way. It's the collective consciousness at work, for good and bad.

I've always felt that some politicians and other so-called leaders are created from this concept. They're often sprung from the darker parts of our collective thoughts. Years upon years of destructive, negative, greedy, and jealous thinking manifests a physical essence in the shape of almost comic-book-style characters who, for some reason or another, seemingly take control, get worshipped by brainless followers, and are encouraged to behave even more as they're expected to behave. This is true across the entire political and religious spectrum, and we're all looking at them—some of us with disgust and some with awe. The observer is the observed, as Krishnamurti often stated. We're all the same, and we've let reality out of our control.

Is all of this just delusion, a distortion of the mind? No, I don't feel it's so. It is a "real reality," no matter how we see it, that belongs in human nature—even with its sometimes disturbing conclusions. The thing is, we are in control and we don't know it. We've let the cat out of the bag, and now it's roaming wild with fully extracted claws and its eyes set on our precious newly bought IKEA sofa.

The phenomenon, all of it, is a part of us. It wants to be seen; it wants us to react and respond, like a naughty child craving the cookie jar on top of the shelf.

"... it is as puzzling as it is fascinating; since, despite all observations I know of, there is no certainty about their very nature. On the other side, there is overwhelming material pointing to their legendary or mythological aspect. As a matter of fact, the psychological aspect is so impressive that one almost must regret that the UFOs seem to be real after all," psychotherapist Carl Jung wrote in a 1957 letter to the *New Republic*. In his book,

Flying Saucers: A Modern Myth of Things Seen in the Skies (1959), he expands on the subject and puts forth several possibilities—including that the phenomenon is something very natural and has always been visible to mankind but still has no true physical connection to Earth and its inhabitants.

I'm always getting back to the intelligent playfulness of it all, the trickster personality in many of the incidents on the fringe of UFO culture. Too few dare to go there because of the stigma within the stigma. One can say it's fine today to accept the possibility of UAPs but not a psychic connection of levitating cubes, as the latter just seems to be too out there in comparison. A UAP can be, for what we know, a spy drone or secret military technology flying around, not known to even those who should know —especially in a country like the United States, which has built its whole foundation on secrecy.

A human experience somewhere on a dark country road is by any means a real human experience—no matter how it's perceived by the person present. The videos "leaked by government officials are only copies of experiences, digitized versions of events that can never be as real as someone actually telling about them. The stories told by fighter pilots are in these cases of importance, even if they're conditioned by their background: enemy or not enemy, threat or not threat. It's not the underlying experience of being human in a mysterious, almost mystic and profound situation. I'm generalizing a bit, as I'm sure even the most hardcore, tough, and patriotic officials can have profound experiences, but the involvement of those higher up on the ladder of power will always lurk in the shadows.

That's why I'm always coming back to the personal, nonofficial, and intimate experiences of people like you and me. In Sweden—a traditionally very secular country—this is unique, especially when it comes to those cases with a high strangeness factor. I can't say what Kjell, Knut, Jörgen, Ulrika, Lilli-Ann, Rune, Ante, Benny, Jan, and the others really experienced. I'm not the one to judge. One can speculate, but judgment doesn't belong here.

What I'll always do, as always when I've been researching unexplained phenomena, is to accept and respect the stories being told. In my humble opinion, their personal experience is always more important than physical proof and thorough investigations. What I do believe, though, is that something is flying around up there, things that come knocking on the door with gifts and want to play a game of mischief.

Imagine you're underwater, swimming among coral reefs, or maybe in a pool somewhere. You're almost levitating down there, and all is calm. The water is embracing you, and if it weren't for us humans missing that important physical and biological talent of breathing during those conditions, it would seem completely normal, like up on dry ground. I see the phenomenon like that; it's always around—but we're not completely comfortable with it because of how we are constructed. I tend to see the concept of it all as a natural phenomenon. Just like everything else in our nature, it exists to challenge us. It wakes us up when life becomes routine, it makes us challenge our belief systems. It teases us. It makes us come alive, no matter what it is.

Let's put UFOs under an umbrella together with Bigfoot, ghosts, psychic powers, and other kinds of unexplained mysteries. It's all the same, just with different appearances depending on who's studying it. As stated above, the observer is the observed. We're looking at ourselves, and ourselves are looking back at us. What we see is a dreamlike reflection of our own past, a perception viewed through the experiences and information we've consciously or unconsciously received since we were born. It doesn't mean it's not true; it's a reality of its own. Like water, earth, fire, and air, there's another, partly unseen element that some of us see, but everyone, in one way or another, interacts with. The medieval science and ancients called it Aether; the chaos magicians say it's one of the five directions of the pentagram: "the material that fills the region of the universe beyond the terrestrial sphere" (a quote from the not always so infinite wisdom of Wikipedia).

In that element, everything can happen, and all kinds of experiences can be produced—always in connection with our consciousness, even physical in parts. It is a mystery, a riddle that we might never solve. Maybe it's for the best.

Ivar Naumann had just lit his pipe and was contemplating the book he had been reading in the kitchen. It's past midnight in the cabin he and his wife had rented for the summer of 1958. She's asleep, but Ivar, deeply focused on reading, couldn't put the book down. Suddenly, he saw someone move near the outhouse. At first, he thought it was a neighbor, a farmer named Oskar, and didn't think much about it. Ivar took a puff on the pipe again and continued to read but was overcome by the feeling that someone was watching him. He looked outside the window again, and to his shock, no less than fifty centimeters away, someone was observing him: "It was too dark outside for me to notice the skin color, but it was lighter than the helmet and coverall. The eyes appeared somewhat larger than human eyes and were completely black. His gaze had an unexplained effect; it hypnotized me." Ivar rushed outside and started to chase the childlike entity, until he came to a wheat field where the visitor climbed up the ladder of what best could be described as a typical flying saucer standing on three legs. The craft took off and left a stunned Ivar on the ground.

"You must have been dreaming!" his wife later told him, but the day after, he found three deep impressions in the field and the vegetation pressed down in a circular shape exactly twelve meters in diameter.

Was it a dream? Was it a creation of the focused mind of Ivar? Or maybe something else, a visitor from an unknown physical or nonphysical place in our universe? One thing is for sure, Ivar—like so many others—was surrounded by silence, deep in his own mind. Focused and calm, and thereby open to the unexpected.

Our consciousness is a whole universe by itself, a sparkling mind sky of infinite stars. Of course, we're not alone there. One day, a strange visitor might come knocking on your existence with a delicious gift.

The question will be, as it always has been, if you will accept it or not.

sources

Watch Out, It's Not Human!

Sven Schalin's original report of the incident, September 19, 1967
"Monster report from Sweden" (The A.P.R.O. Bulletin, September-October, 1967)
"Rymdbesök eller vad?" (Sven Schalin, *Sökaren*, issue 1, 1968)
"Was this creature a visitor from Space" (*Saucers, Space & Science*, issue 53, 1968)
"Liten tefatsman skrämde 15-åringar" (*UFO-Information*, issue 6, 1973)
"Psychological Aspects of the Alien Contact Experience" (Christopher C. French, Julia Santomauro, Victoria Hamilton, Rachel Fox, p. 5–6, 2008)
"Humanoidfall från 1967 ännu utan förklaring" (*UFO-Aktuellt*, issue 2, 2017)
"Tolv små män med grymma drag kom emot mig i månskensnatten" (Anders Liljegren, *UFO-Information*, issue 2, 1973)
The Hidden Universe (Anthony Peake, p. 95, 2019)

Underground Humanoids

Conversation with Benny Magnusson conducted by the author 25/5/2022.
"Humanoider i Dalarna: Benny och hans kompisar såg jättelika varelser sväva över marken" (*Hårda Tider*, issue 6-7, 1994)
Kontakt med UFO! (Boris Jungkvist, p. 130–131, 1994)
"Fältforskare undersöker trollgrottor i Dalarna" (*Avesta Tidning*, Jan-Olov Sundberg, 16/5/1974)
"High Strangeness, the Oz Factor and Symbols" (Fred Andersson, Medium.com, 2022)
Dimensions: A Casebook of Alien Contact (Jacques Vallée, 1988)
Evolutionary Metaphors (David J. Moore, 2019)

Boxes

"UFO-besättning besökte svensk länkstation" (Jan-Ove Sundberg and Anders Liljegren, *UFO-Information*, issue 6, 1972)
"Närkontakt av tredje graden med humanoider i Ångermanland" (Carl-Anton Mattsson and Thorvald Berthelsen, *UFO-Information*, issue 1, 1978)
"Närkontakt Havedalen" (Arne Lundberg and det Carl-Anton Mattsson, *UFO-Aktuellt*, issue 1, 1985)

UFO-mysteriet: från flygande tefat till cirklar i sädesfält (Clas Svahn, Parthenon, 1998)
UFO spökraketer, ljusglober och utomjordingar (Clas Svahn, Semic, 2014)
Letter from Kjell Näslund to UFO-Örnsköldsvik/Ragnar Söderberg plus follow-up interview.

Frogmen in Black

The Complete Secret Cipher of the UFOnauts (Allen H. Greenfield, 2018)
Alien Dawn (Colin Wilson, p. 124–125, 1999)
"Exorcism and UFO Landing at Loch Ness" (F. W. Holiday, *Flying Saucer Review*, #5, 1973)
"False Report from Loch Ness" (Stuart Campbell, *Flying Saucer Review*, #6, 1981)
"Jan-Ove Sundberg" (Jan-Ove Sundberg, Paranormal.se)
"What Happened to Bevan Berthelsen" (Håkan Blomqvist, 2014)
"Berthelsen fick UFO-Sverige att växa" (Håkan Blomqvist, 1991)
"Men in Black: Hallucinationer hos dårfinkar eller hemliga agenter?" (Lars B. Lindholm, *Pentagram*, #3, 1995)
Fantomubåtarna (Jan-Ove Sundberg, p. 103–112, 1993)
"'Texas' Sundbergs fantastiska värld" (Sven Magnusson, *Sökaren*, #9, 1984)
A Self-Induced Hallucination (Jane Schoenbrun, 2018)
"Memes in Black" (Fred Andersson, Medium.com, 2020)

Night of the UFOs

Conversation with Hillevi Andersson conducted by the author 30/11/2020.
"Händelserna i Vallentuna 1974" (Clas Svahn, UFO-Sweden)
"DN om Vallentunavågen – NewsVoice har detaljerna" (Torbjörn Sassersson, NewsVoice, 21/3/2014)
"Vallentunafallet – en gåta som väntar på lösning" (Håkan Blomqvist, *UFO-Aktuellt*, issue 1, 2011)
"Hundratals rapporter om föremål över Vallentuna" (Håkan Blomqvist, *UFO-Aktuellt*, issue 2, 2011)
"Ufo-gåtan i Vallentuna ännu ej löst – Hillevi minns dagen 1974" (Uffe Lindeborg, *Mitt i Vallentuna*, 23/3/2017)
Alien Dawn: An Investigation into the Contact Experience (Colin Wilson, Virgin Publishing Ltd, p. 201–203, 1998)

When a Flying Saucer Landed at Lake Anten: A Look into Alleged UFO Landings in Sweden

"UFO-landing vid Anten?" (Editorial department and Lloyd Simu, *UFO-Information*, #10, 1970)
"Uppföljning av Anten-fallet" (Alf Tollhag, *GICOFF-Information*, #4, 1971)
"Märkena vid Enebacken" (Editorial department, *GICOFF-Information*, #1, 1971)
"Tre runda hål förbryllar..." (Philip Mauritzson, *Alingsås Tidning*, January 3, 2017)
"Cirklar i Snön" (*GICOFF-Information*, #4, 1971)
"En Landning vid Skirsjön" (Håkan Blomqvist, *UFO-Bladet*, #1, 1972)
"Skirenfallet – kommentarer och tillägg" (Anders Liljegren, *Ufologen*, #11, 1973)
"UFO över Dalabygd" (Christer Dahlstedt & Niels Nielsen, *UFO-Information*, #11, 1979)
"1968 Landade ett Okänt Föremål i Vänga?" (Jörgen Granlie, UFO-Sverige, ufo.se)
UFO! Nya Fakta om de Flygande Tefaten (K. Gösta Rehn, p. 33–34, Zindermans, 1969)
The Johansson Family and Enebacken on WikiTree.

The Boys

Original case file/UFO-Sverige 11/2/1978
UFO-Mysteriet: Från Flygande Tefat till Cirklar i Sädesfälten (Clas Svahn, p. 115–117, Parthenon, 1998)
UFO – spökraketer, ljusglober och utomjordingar (Clas Svahn, p. 207–209, Semic, 2014)
"Pojkar på spark lyfte och försvann" (*UFO-Information*, issue 1, 1979)
"Närkontakter i Norrland" (Clas Svahn, *UFO-Aktuellt*, issue 4, 1985)
"Positive Magnetic Anomalies and Electron Diffusion Regions in Association with UAP" (Barry Fitzgerald and Steve Mera, 2019)
The Eighth Tower: On Ultraterrestrials and the Superspectrum (John A. Keel, 1975)
"Mystiska figurer lekte med ljussignaler" (Carl-Axel Jonzon, *UFO-Aktuellt*, issue 6, 1980)
"Närkontakt Havedalen" (Arne Lundberg and det Carl-Anton Mattsson, *UFO-Aktuellt*, issue 1, 1985
"Utomjordiska varelser på nattlig spaningstur i Mantorp" (*UFO-Information*, issue 3, 1973)

Strangers with Candy

"Närkontakt med Västervik" (Tor Wiklund, *UFO-Information*, issue 4, 1980)
Email conversation with photographer and investigator Tor Wiklund, 2022.

Sources

"Mystisk nattlig upplevelse: Närkontakt med Västervik" (*Västerviks-Tidningen*, issue 221, 1980)

A Trojan Feast: The Food and Drink Offerings of Aliens, Faeries, and Sasquatch (Joshua Cutchin, 2015)

Besök Hos Utomjordiska Civilisationer (Sune Hjort, 1989)

The original 1759 account by Jacob Jacobsson, written down by Rev. Vigelius.

Wonders in the Sky: Unexplained Aerial Objects from Antiquity to Modern Times (Jacques Vallée & Chris Aubeck, p. 223–224, 2010)

The Unidentified: Notes Towards Solving the UFO Mystery (Jerome Clarke & Loren Coleman, p. 70–71, 1975)

Danaiderna: Ett försök att förstå UFO-fenomenet (Staffan Andersson, Parthenon, 1999)

Passport to Magonia: From Folklore to Flying Saucers (Jacques Vallée, 1969)

Reality Shift

"Bilen försvann framför oss" (Carl-Anton Mattsson, *UFO-Aktuellt*, issue 3, 1981)

Original case file/UFO-Sverige 28/6/1981.

Conversation with Jan Kerbosch 17/3/2022 conducted by the author 30/11 2020.

"The Car That Disappeared" (Jenny Randles and Derek James, *Flying Saucer Review*, vol. 23, issue 3, 1977)

UFO Reality (Jenny Randles, p. 100, 1983)

Time Storms: The Amazing Evidence of Time Warps, Space Rifts & Time Travel (Jenny Randles, 2001)

Email from Göran Andersson, October 15, 2022.

Aliens Attack!

Earths in the Universe (Emanuel Swedenberg, 1758)

UFO – spökraketer, ljusglober och utomjordingar (Clas Svahn, Semic, p. 252–264, 2014)

"Närkontakt av tredje graden i Småland" (Håkan Sterner, issue 1, 1985)

"Ingen kan förklara" (Torsten Lindberg, *Kvällposten*, 22/11/1984)

Messengers of Deception: UFO Contacts and Cults (Jacques Vallée, 1979)

"Sten Lindgren och rymdbröderna" (Håkan Blomqvist, UFO.se)

Sektledaren Mor Lilly (Joanna Górecka, *P3 Dokumentär*, 2022)

"Här har det ju alltid spökat" (Peter Carlberg, *Kronobergaren*, 26/11/1984)

Ante Jonsson – Besök hos utomjordiska civilisationer (Ante Jonsson and Sune Hjort, Zindermans Förlag, 1989)

Främlingar på vår Jord (Håkan Blomqvist, p. 34–37, Parthenon, 2009)

"Plåtburkar eller andar" (Håkan Blomqvist, *Sökaren*, issue 10, 1985)

"UFOs in the Sture Johansson Channeling" (Håkan Blomqvist, Håkan Blomqvist's blog, March 30, 2018)

Like the Wings of a Dragonfly

Conversation with Ulrika and Jörgen Berg conducted by the author 11/1/2022.
UFO-Mysteriet: Från Flygande Tefat till Cirklar i Sädesfälten (Clas Svahn, Parthenon Förlag, p. 125–128, 1998)
UFO – spökraketer, ljusglober och utomjordingar (Clas Svahn, Semic, p. 252–264, 2014)
"Self-replicating spacecraft" (Wikipedia)
"Märkligt UFO i Göteborgs-trakten" (Stig Aggestad, *UFO-Aktuellt*, issue 2, 1981)
"'Fisk-silhuett' på UFO vid svensk-finska gränsen" (Matlaa Päätola Oulu, *GICOFF-Information*, issue 4, 1976)
"Lysande undervattensobjekt i Torshällaån" (Stig Aggestad, *UFO-Information*, issue 3, 1979)
"Närkontakt Haverdalen" (Arne Lundberg and Carl-Anton Mattsson, *UFO-Aktuellt*, issue 1, 1985)
"Jag stod i sommarstugan och såg ett tefat landa på ängen!" (Björn H. Larsson, *Hemmets Journal*, issue 26, 1985)

Owls and UFOs

Lt. Gustav Nilsson's original report (letter to Royal Swedish Air Force Materiel Administration, September 28, 1952)
"Flygande tefan kan vara meteorer, billjus i uppförsbacke, radarhägring" (*Dagens Nyheter*, October 10, 1952)
"Jag såg djävulen" (Per-Ola Jonasson, *Smålandsposten*, August 8, 1987)
"Esotericism and UFO Research: A Selection and Compilation of Blog Entries 2013–2017" (https://www.ufo.se/images/UFO/pdf/EsotericismandUFOResearch.pdf)
Reader's letter (*Galaxen*, issue 1, 1998)
"200 människor har kidnappats av rymdvarelser" (newspaper clipping from unknown Swedish magazine, reproduced in *UFO-Nytt*, issue 1, 1989)
Danaiderna: Ett försök att förstå UFO-fenomenet (Staffan Andersson, Parthenon, 1999)

Invitation to Play

Original case file/UFO-Sverige 14/2/1989
"Humanoid i Jämtland" (Kurt Persson and Clas Svahn, *UFO-Aktuellt*, issue 2, 1989)
"Närkontakter i Norrland" (Clas Svahn, *UFO-Aktuellt*, issue 4, 1985)
"Vättar anklagas för mystiska olyckor på E4" (Anton Kasurinen, *Arbetarbladet*, January 30, 2015)

"Mystiskt lyktgubbe sprider skräck" (*Norrköpings Tidningar*, August 22, p. 13, 1946)
"The Well-Ordered Abduction: Pattern or Mirage?" (Thomas E. Bullard, included in *Alien Discussions: Proceedings of the Abduction Study Conference*, North Cambridge Press, 1994)
"Lång figur med gula ögon skrämde cyklist" (Anders Berglund & Tage Bång, *UFO-Aktuellt*, issue 3, 2017)

What About That Dead Humanoid in Sweden?

"July 1955, Vestra, Norrland, Sweden, Three Lumberjacks" (Patrik Gross, PDF file, URECAT)
"Alien Dies in Sweden" (John La Fontaine, *UFO Universe Magazine*, August/September 1991)
"Avled en man från en annan planet i Norrland år 1955?" (John La Fontaine, *UFO-Information*, issue 6, 1977)
"UFONAUT i Sverige" (John La Fontaine, *UFO-Aspekt*, issue 4, 1977)
Email conversation with Steen Landsy, June 2022.
The Shocking Truth (Albert Coe, 1969)

Borderlands

"Oförklarliga Möten" (*Historier från Hälsingland*, episode 20, 2018)
"Carl Jung's Fascinating 1957 Letter on UFOs" (Colin, Marshall, openculture.com, May 31, 2013)
Saucers and Saucerers (Allen H. Greenfield, The Celestial Lodge of Sirius, 2022)
"Närkontakter i Norrland" (Clas Svahn, *UFO-Aktuellt*, issue 4, 1985)
"Övernaturligt i naturen" (*Fiskekompisen*, episode 117, 2020)
"Närkontakt av Tredje Graden?" (Set Mattsson, *Allers*, issue 32, 2000)
UFO-Mysteriet: Från Flygande Tefat till Cirklar i Sädesfälten (Clas Svahn, Parthenon Förlag, p. 113–115, 1998)
"Science, Gaia and Archetypes with Darwin" (*6 Degrees of John Keel*, episode 82, 2022)
Communion (Whitley Strieber, Avon, 1987)
Theoretical Weirdo (John E. L. Tenney, p. 105106. 2020)

The Stigma Within the Stigma

Letter to the New Republic (Carl Jung, 1957)
"The New Republic." *In his book Flying Saucers: A Modern Myth of Things Seen in the Skies* (Carl Jung, 1959)

Sources

"Aether (classical element)" (Wikipedia)
"The humanoid that got away" (Håkan Blomqvist, personal blog post, 2014)

about the author

Fred Andersson is a renowned researcher, television freelancer, author, and podcaster in Sweden. With a focus on high strangeness, the paranormal, and UFOs, Fred has carved a niche for himself as an out-of-the-box thinker and explorer of the weird. As a researcher, Fred has appeared on countless international podcasts, written articles on the subject of Swedish high strangeness, and been a guest on radio, magazines, and newspapers.

In his role as a television freelancer, Fred has worked on various award-winning documentaries and programs with a paranormal theme, including hit shows like Det Okända and Spökjakt. As part of a talented team, Fred has contributed to the success of these projects, which have received recognition at the television gala Kristallen. The team's efforts have led to them being honored with the Kristallen audience choice award three times.

As a podcaster, Fred co-hosts 'Märklighetsfaktorn,' where he explores the latest weird news and mysteries from all over the world. He's also involved in UFO-Sverige, an organization that focuses on the study and investigation of UFOs and related phenomena. It is one of the oldest and most prominent UFO research organizations in Sweden.

Throughout his career, Fred has been recognized for his outstanding achievements, and he attributes this success to the collaborative spirit and collective effort of the teams he has worked with. Beyond his professional pursuits, Fred enjoys finding inspiration for his work in weird books, genre films, and spending time in nature.

For updates on his latest projects, connect with Fred on Instagram and Twitter under the account name HomoSatanis or visit his website at www.fredandersson.se.

www.ingramcontent.com/pod-product-compliance
Lightning Source LLC
LaVergne TN
LVHW050958080826
845145LV00009B/2339

* 9 7 8 1 9 5 4 5 2 8 7 2 7 *